Getting
GREAT
Guitar
Sounds

GORDON PRICE MUSIC LTD.
10828 Whyte Avenue
EDMONTON, ALBERTA T6E 2B3
(403) 439-0007

Getting GREAT Guitar Sounds

A non-technical approach to developing, controlling, and shaping your own personal sound

by
Michael Ross

HAL LEONARD BOOKS

ISBN 0-88188-596-7

For my wife, Nancy, "Everybody needs an editor."

ACKNOWLEDGEMENTS

Since I did not make up all this information nor learn it all from my own experience, I would like to gratefully acknowledge the people who allowed me to draw from their knowledge and experience: Mike Matthews former president of Electro-Harmonix Inc., Rudy Pensa and John Suhr of Rudy's Music Stop N.Y., NY, Gary Brawer of Stringed Instrument Repair, San Francisco, CA, and Paul Chandler of Chandler Industries, San Francisco, CA.

This book would have been all text had it not been for the kind help of the following people who provided pictures and illustrations: Milt Williams, Bob Benedetto, Rudy's Music Stop, Steve Kaufman at E.S.P.(Shibuya Enterprises Inc.), Seymour Duncan, DOD (Digitech), Ibanez (Hoshino Inc.), Alesis, Chandler Industries, and Scholz (Rockman).

Finally, I would like to thank the guitarists whose sound influenced and inspired me over the years. In no particular order they are: James Burton, Steve Cropper, Jim Hall, Eric Clapton, Jeff Beck, Buddy Guy, Cornell Dupree, the King family (Albert, B.B., and Freddy), Amos Garrett, Buzzy Feiten, Robben Ford, Bill Frisell, Larry Carlton, Robbie Robertson, Roy Buchannan, Billy Butler, Adrian Belew, Alan Murphy, and last, but not least, my brother Norman.

CONTENTS

Introduction

What Is "Great" Guitar Sound

"Great" sound is obviously a subjective term. What you might consider a great sound someone else might call an awful noise (remember parents and rock music?). Therefore if we are going to spend an entire book discussing great guitar sounds, we had should begin by defining what we mean.

For our purposes, great sound could be described as sound that allows the guitarist to express him or herself as fully as possible. Pat Metheney and Edward Van Halen sound not at all alike, but each has developed a personal sound that allows him to communicate his musical ideas and feelings with maximum efficiency. It is unlikely that Van Halen's distorted sound would be appropriate for Metheney's lyrical excursions, nor would Pat's spacey chiming be right for Eddie's hell-bent-for-leather boogie. Both guitarists are virtuoso technicians, but it is more than fast fingers and great ideas that set them above the crowd—it is the proper use of modern electronic technology that has helped their music capture the imagination of millions of listeners.

We could say, then, that great sound is controlled sound—distorted when you want it, clean when that is called for, up front when you need it, distant and spacey when appropriate. It is the purpose of this book to help you to control your sound and shape it to your needs as an individual.

Once you understand the principles of sound herein you should be able to achieve any guitar sound you desire. You will know what equipment you need to copy any guitar sound that you hear on record. It is my profound hope, however, that copying records will not be your goal. I would rather that you use the information in this book to help you develop a sound that is uniquely your own. Experience will show you (if it hasn't already) that when you hear yourself play with a sound you consider "great," you will play your best—which is, after all, what it's all about.

PART

ONE

The
Guitar

CHAPTER 1
The Electric Guitar as an Acoustic Instrument

IT IS A COMMON MISCONCEPTION that an electric guitar is "just a frame holding some pickups, and it is the pickups that create the sound." If this were true we could begin our discussion of great guitar sounds with Chapter Two. However, this is not the case. A great sounding guitar must sound great before being plugged in or, for that matter, before any pickups are installed.

G.E. Smith (guitarist for *Hall and Oates, Saturday Night Live,* Mick Jagger, etc.) once came into a music store where I was working to buy some strings and such. While I was calling in for his credit card verification number, he asked to see a guitar that was on display. He strummed it once, listened and said, "Put it on the card." This was not to impress me with his wealth. It was because as an ex-guitar salesman and experienced collector, he could tell from that one strum that the guitar sounded great acoustically, and therefore had the potential to sound great electrically. I say "potential" because obviously bad pickups could diminish the sound, but it is important to remember—*an electric guitar that does not sound great acoustically will never sound great electrically.* With great pickups, a multitude of effects, and a great amp, a guitar that sounds bad acoustically can be made to sound good, but not *great*—and great sound is what we are after.

Why? The elusive characteristics of a great sounding guitar—tone, sustain, warmth, resonance and the ability to cut through the sound of the rest of the band—all start with the acoustic instrument. The materials chosen and the way they are put together will determine many of the sound characteristics of the guitar.

HOW AN ELECTRIC GUITAR WORKS

Basically, an electric guitar transmits the sound of vibrating strings through the pickups to an amplifier and out of the speakers to your ears. The most obvious part of the sound that is transmitted is the pitch. Whether and where the string is fretted will determine what note is heard. Less obviously, the vibrating string transmits tonal qualities. Some of these tonal qualities are determined by the pickup type and placement and some by the makeup of the string itself. But—**and this is important**—*it also transmits the tonal quality of the guitar as an acoustic instrument.* If you strum an unplugged electric guitar that sounds thin and tinny and the notes decay and die rapidly, this is how it will sound when plugged in. Conversely, if it sounds full and fat acoustically and the notes seem to ring endlessly, this will contribute to the sound coming out of the amplifier.

Many factors affect the acoustic tone of an electric guitar. The following is a discussion of some of them. While absorbing this information keep one thing in mind: When all is said and done, guitars are like people. Think of identical twins—same parents, same environment, but they can be as different as night and day. Guitars are the same—you can have the same person build two guitars out of the same materials and they will sound very different. Why this is should become clearer as you read on.

Before we get into specifics, let me reveal a bias on my part. In recent years guitar manufacturers have come up with necks and bodies made of graphite compounds (Modulous Graphite, Steinberger) and metal (Gitler, Travis Bean). These materials offer some advantages over wood. Graphite compounds are more stable than wood, and are less likely to shift over the years or with seasonal, regional, or other temperature extremes. Metal guitars can offer unique designs, like the tubular Gitler guitar currently on permanent exhibit at the New York Museum of Modern Art. Both materials offer an evenness of frequency response and no "dead spots" (places on the neck where the note decays faster). Nevertheless, it is my opinion that for individuality of tone and maximum personal expression, no one has come up with anything that surpasses the well made wooden electric guitar.

This is not mere nostalgia on my part, nor only personal prejudice. In interview after interview with famous musicians like Marcus Miller, bassist with Miles Davis, or Bruce Thomas, bassist with Elvis Costello, they talk about building their styles around the dead spots on their Fender basses. Even Steinberger has brought out a wooden model for "those who prefer the feel of wood."

Graphite compounds and metal tubing may be wonders of man's technology, but "only God can make a tree." Like snowflakes, no two trees are exactly alike—not even two parts of the same tree are exactly alike. These variations result in each wooden guitar having it's own personality, and the combination of it's personality and yours is what allows great music to be made.

HEADSTOCKS

Much of the guitar's resonance is transmitted through the headstock. You need only to grip the headstock of a guitar in your left hand and strum it with your right (reverse for lefties) to feel the vibrations. Thus, wooden "headless" guitars sacrifice a significant amount of sustain (graphite compound ones, like the Steinberger, make it up in the properties of the graphite itself).

That said, the actual shape of the headstock has little effect on the tone. More important is how the headstock affects the tension of the strings across the nut.

Early acoustic and electric acoustic (archtop) guitars had headstocks with three tuning gears per side. (By "early," I mean from the turn of the century until the fifties.) These headstocks were also tilted at an angle away from the fingerboard in order to maintain the all important tension across the nut. To hear how this tension affects the sound, try taking the high E string on a Fender guitar out from under the string tree that holds it down. (The string tree is located between the nut and the tuning gear.) Tune it up to pitch. Listen carefully to the sound. Now loosen the string and place it back under the string tree. Tune it to pitch and listen again. The sound should be much fuller and less tinny.

The "three on a side" headstock configuration still exists on most acoustic guitars and Gibson style electric guitars, but it has two basic disadvantages:

One: In addition to being pulled at an angle across the nut (which is good), the strings are pulled at an angle against the side of the nut (which is bad). This angle can cause tuning problems, especially when bending strings. (That is probably why, tradition aside, this headstock still remains popular in acoustic guitars where string bending is less prevalent.)

Two: The player must turn the bottom tuners in a different direction than the top ones to achieve the same effect. This can prove confusing in the middle of a song when a quick tuning touch up is necessary.

A beautifully inlaid archtop headstock by luthier Bob Benedetto.

Along came Leo Fender in the early fifties to popularize the "six in line" style headstock with all the gears on top. Note that I say "popularize" and not invent. Mr. Bigsby had built a six in line headstock a few years previously, and there are even some ancient relatives of the guitar with a similar design. Nonetheless, Leo had the right idea at the right time. The growing popularity of string bending made this design very desirable. Why? Because the six in line design allows the strings to pass straight through the nut to the tuning machines without any side angles to throw the string out of tune. However, the headstock was not angled back from the nut. This allowed Fender to make a one piece neck from a smaller piece of wood, and thus produce more affordable guitars. Unfortunately, it necessitates the use of one or more string trees, or retainers, to maintain the tension across the nut. This is unfortunate because these string trees can cause the same tuning problem we were trying to eliminate. We will see how to eliminate this problem in the next section.

Recent years have seen the rise in popularity of two new styles of six in line headstocks: The Charvel or Jackson style, which tilts back but does not allow the strings to pass straight to the tuners, and the Kramer or Explorer style, which does neither. The tuning problems presented by these headstocks are usually rendered academic by the use of a locking nut system.

TUNING MACHINES AND TUNING

The type of tuning machines that you use on your instrument can affect the sound, if somewhat indirectly. Some tuning machines have very high posts. In a Fender type headstock, this can cause insufficient tension across the nut, which can be fixed by using two or three string trees to hold the strings down. This solution is less than ideal because these string trees can catch the string, causing it to go out of tune especially when using a vibrato system. A much better answer is to use tuners with low enough posts to offer proper tension using only one string tree or, even better, none. The tuners should still be high enough to allow two or three windings to keep the string from popping out. Some companies offer what are known as "staggered" tuners; that is, tuners with posts that get lower as the strings get higher.

When stringing the guitar, the amount of windings around the posts is critical. You need enough to prevent the string from pulling loose and enough windings going down the post to create the proper tension across the nut. However, many times a player will put too many windings on the peg. This causes the string to wind back up the post, thereby reducing the tension. In addition, as the strings are played these windings continually tighten, causing the strings to go flat or, if the vibrato arm is depressed, the windings loosen and when the arm is released, the string is sharp. Two to five windings are normally sufficient, depending on the height of the post and the thickness of the string. Locking tuning machines lock the string into the post, removing the need for any windings—just be sure that the posts are low enough to provide proper tension.

Hint: When players have a guitar that is difficult to keep in tune, the first thing they assume is that a tuning gear is slipping. In a twenty to thirty year old instrument with the original tuners, this may be the reason. But even then, you should first check: Your windings (too many), your strings (too old), your intonation (see the section on setup), your finger pressure (see "frets"). If all of these are in order, *then* it might be the tuning gears.

THE NUT

The thin piece of material (either bone, graphite, or brass) between the headstock and the fretboard is called the "nut." The effect that the type of nut material used has on the tone of the guitar is often overestimated. More frequently the importance of a well cut nut is underestimated. The tone of a bone nut may be marginally different than a brass, graphite, or chromed metal locking nut, but far more importantly, a guitar with a badly cut nut will never play as well or ring as true as one with an expertly cut nut. It is vital that the strings pass through this portion of the guitar without binding or flopping around. And, as we discussed earlier, the tension of the strings across this part of the instrument has everything to do with its tone. If the strings are improperly seated, they will not vibrate properly and great sound is impossible.

Cutting a nut properly requires a set of variously sized files, much patience, two or three nut blanks (to replace the ones that you mess up), and years of experience. If you lack any or all of the above, you may want a qualified professional to do it. As with fret jobs, be prepared to pay for a top job. A professional may charge what seems like a lot of money to cut some notches, but remember that a bargain is not a bargain if your strings pop out, or stop ringing almost immediately, or get caught in the nut when you use the vibrato arm.

My personal preference is for a well cut bone or synthetic bone nut. Brass nuts were a trend for a while for reasons that have been dimmed by history. Graphite nuts are self-lubricating, theoretically allowing the string to pass through more easily. Keep in mind, however, that graphite is more difficult to work with than bone, and you are better off with a well cut bone nut than with a poorly cut graphite one. Locking nuts come in two basic varieties: (a) Those that go behind the existing nut and are screwed into the headstock (Kahler, Wonderbar, etc.); and (b) those that replace the existing nut (Floyd Rose and other nuts that are licensed by them).

For my money—and for yours, too—the ones that go behind the nut are rather pointless and were basically invented to circumvent the Floyd Rose patent. After all, the string still has to pass through the existing nut where it can get caught. The Floyd Rose nut sits where the nut usually sits and avoids any catching problems. This may sound as if I own stock in Floyd Rose Inc., but that is not the case (would that it were!). It is simply that my experience has shown that if you are going to put up with the hassles of a locking system (excessive string changing time, diminished sustain), it would be wise to use a system that *(properly installed!)* has the best track record for staying in tune.

FRETS

The twenty-one to twenty-four metal strips across the neck of a guitar are known as "frets." In addition to affecting playability and intonation, frets can also affect the sound. Uneven or badly worn frets can cause buzzing, fretting out (the sound cuts off sharply), and poor intonation (the guitar may play in tune in some positions but not in others). Frets come in different heights and widths, and the theories concerning the best size have changed as playing styles have changed. In the end, it all comes down to personal preference, but here is some information that may help you determine what size frets will best fit *your* own style of playing.

Original Fender frets were thin and relatively low. They did the job (and still do) for strumming and standard jazz or flat picking. Early players were accustomed to higher actions and heavy gauge strings that they rarely bent. Early Gibsons introduced wider (but still low) frets, claiming greater sustain from the metal-to-metal contact of string and fret. It is more likely that the increased sustain of guitars like the Les Paul came from their heavier bodies (more on bodies later), but it is a fact that wide frets create intonation problems, since they do not provide a clear cut-off point for the string.

Later on (in the late sixties), higher frets became popular. Players wanted low action for speed, but also the ability to get their fingers under the frets for bending. It became common to replace Fender frets with higher frets to compensate for the rounder radius of the early Fender fretboards (see Figure 1). This round radius tends to make the high E and B strings "choke," or cut-off, as they are bent into the center "hump" of the radius. This can be avoided by raising the action, but higher frets help the string over the hump without raising the action as high. Today fingerboards are more commonly flattened either at the factory or when new frets are installed.

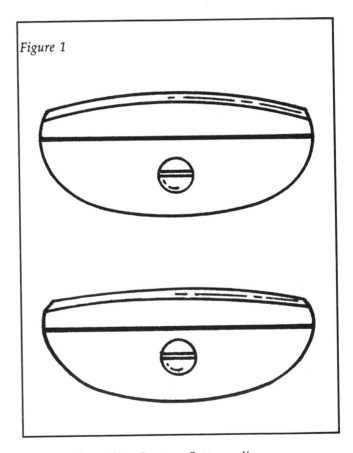

Figure 1

Top: rounder radius. Bottom: flatter radius.

As of this writing, a current favorite is high, thin frets allowing easy bending, low action and good intonation. Your personal style of playing should determine which frets are right for you. For example, if your style involves sliding into notes, you may find high frets uncomfortable. Or, if you have big fingers, you may find that wide frets do not leave you enough fingerboard room at the twelfth fret and beyond. Try different instruments with frets of varying shapes and sizes to see what is most comfortable and compatible with your style of playing.

Hint: High frets require a lighter touch than lower frets. This is because when you press the string against the fret, the proper note is sounded as soon as the string makes firm contact. Further pressure causes the note to go sharp, which may be hard to tell when playing single notes. However if you play a chord and some notes are out of tune, you may be pushing harder with those fingers (this assumes that the guitar is in tune, is properly intonated, and the frets are even).

This is probably as good a place as any to discuss scalloped necks. Neck scalloping refers to depressions that are cut into the fingerboard between the frets, in effect creating super-high frets. In theory, this allows increased expressive possibilities: i.e. enhanced vibrato, bending and speed. In practice, it makes playing in tune very difficult—anything but the exact amount of finger pressure will make the note slightly sharp (too much pressure) or flat (too little pressure). The guitar virtuosos who play scalloped necks (Larry Carlton, John McLaughlin, Yngwie Malmsteen, etc.) have put in many hours of practice to be able to play these instruments in tune. If you must try neck scalloping, consider having it done to an extra guitar so that you can practice on it while playing on a more conventional fingerboard.

Whatever type of frets you choose, it is of first importance that they are even and leveled—that is, that they are all the same height and shape. Wear spots can cause buzzing, choking and intonation problems. Newer frets can be fixed with a "leveling" or "grind and polish." This process involves grinding the higher frets down to the level of the more worn ones and "crowning" them, that is, shaping them into a point so that the string has a well defined place to make contact for proper intonation. The frets are then polished smooth. You may have to adjust your action or neck tension (see "set-up") after a leveling, but you'll find that the guitar will play and sound better with even, well crowned frets. A good fret leveling can even correct minor warps or twists.

Even brand new guitars may need this kind of fret work, unless the guitar is custom made for you by a skilled luthier. Assembly line guitars rarely, if ever, have a proper fret leveling done at the factory. This is because a repair person needs to know something about your playing style to do the job properly.

If your guitar is older and the frets have been leveled too many times, or you just want different frets, or your neck is badly twisted or warped, you may need to replace the frets entirely. This is an exacting, complex job that should ideally be undertaken by a highly qualified repair person. Because of its complexity it can be an expensive job, so before you invest your money, you should consider: Do I love this neck? Do I love the way it feels in my hand? Or, if the fret job is to correct a twist or warp: Will the neck then be stable, or will it twist again? If you have any doubts, you may want to consider buying a new neck (assuming your guitar has a bolt-on, replaceable neck). Replacing the entire neck with one that feels better and/or is more reliable may cost only a little more than replacing the frets alone, and you will have an instrument that makes you much happier.

If you decide that you are satisfied with your current neck, then by all means go ahead with the fret job. First the old frets will be removed. A good luthier will then check to make sure that the fingerboard is straight. It is at this point that bows, backbows (see "necks"), or twists untreatable by heat or fret leveling can be corrected by planing the fingerboard straight. This, however, assumes that there is a thick enough fingerboard to allow planing, which is another factor you should check before deciding whether to have a fret job done or replace the entire neck. You may also have the radius flattened at this point. **(Be careful—bargain fret jobs often cost less because they do not include a fingerboard planing.)** New frets are then carefully inserted and leveled and a new nut is cut. A well fretted guitar will play and sound 100% better than a poorly fretted one.

NECKS

Guitar necks are most often made from one or more of the following woods—maple, rosewood, and ebony. The type of wood used in the neck will affect the sound, but more on that later.

One of the primary considerations when evaluating the neck of a guitar is *stability*; whether the neck will twist and warp over the years or shift excessively with changes in temperature. When wood is "green," or freshly cut, it is still settling. If it is immediately made into a neck, there is no telling what it will do over time.

In the "good old days," wooden instruments, including early electric guitars, were made from wood that was aged after it was cut. Most of the settling process took place before the wood was made into a neck. This is one of the reasons (other than collector value) that older electrics are so highly prized and priced. Another is that if a neck on a twenty or thirty year old instrument was going to warp or twist, it would have done so ten or twenty years ago. If the neck on a fifties Fender is straight now, you can be sure it will remain so.

Today no one has time to age wood naturally, so the wood is "kiln dried"—an artificial aging process that helps increase stability to a certain extent.

Of the commonly used woods, maple is the most frequently used. If the neck is not solid maple or maple with a separate maple fingerboard, the odds are that it is maple with a rosewood or ebony fingerboard. Maple fingerboards offer a brighter sound than rosewood, but tend to wear and discolor. Beware of heavily "flamed" maple necks; they are very attractive, but tend to be more unstable than plainer maple.

Rosewood is most often used only for fingerboards (with a maple base). Solid rosewood necks are beautiful, but they are expensive, heavy, and add little to the sound. Rosewood necks and those with rosewood fingerboards are darker and warmer sounding than maple ones. They wear a little better and absorb finger oils without noticeable discoloring.

often used for fingerboards and it offers the brightness of maple without the wear and discoloration problems.

Exotic woods such as African wenge and Indian laurel can also be used for necks, but while attractive, they offer no particular advantage in sound or stability—there is a reason that the most common woods are the most common.

Even the most stable necks will sometimes shift with extremes of temperature. Therefore, most wood necks will have a metal rod running their length. This rod is either installed before the fingerboard goes on, or in a one piece neck through a groove in the back (these usually have a stripe of contrasting color wood). Turning this rod allows either you or a repair person to straighten the neck if it should shift.

Guitar necks usually shift in one of two ways—bowing or backbowing (see Figure 2). Many would-be experts spend hours sighting down guitar necks from one end or the other to see if they are straight. This is fine, especially if you are purchasing a new neck for your guitar. However, for those of you who are maintaining the guitar you own or are looking to purchase a fully assembled guitar, a more practical approach may be in order. I call it the "if it ain't broke, don't fix it" method.

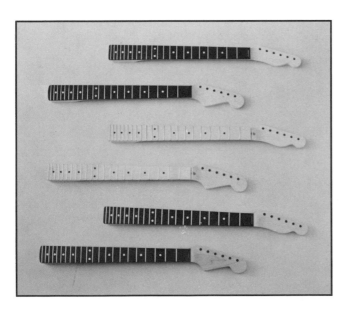

Rosewood and maple, Fender style replacement necks.

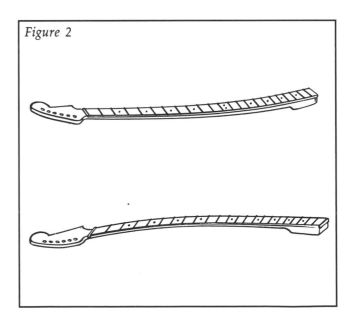

Figure 2

Top: bowed. Bottom: backbowed.

Ebony is very rarely used for an entire neck. It would be prohibitively expensive and very heavy, since ebony is the most costly and the densest of the three woods. However, ebony is

First, set the action of the guitar (the height of the strings above the fingerboard) so that it is comfortable for your playing style in open position. Now play the guitar toward the middle (between the nut and the bridge). If the action seems to get uncomfortably high as you move up the neck, it may be bowed, or as some say, overbowed. In this case, tightening the truss rod is in order. If, however, the action is comfortable down near the nut, but the strings "fret out" (that is, they stop resonating as soon as you press them down), or buzz excessively (meaning audibly through the amp) as you play toward the middle of the neck, the neck may be backbowed. In this case, the truss rod should be loosened. If the truss rod fails to correct the problem, see the chapter on frets and a good repair person—not necessarily in that order.

Most necks should have a slight bow in them to play properly, and "neck sighters" tend to get unduly agitated at anything but a straight line. I have played great sounding guitars with backbows, overbows and twists. Once again, just like people, sometimes a guitar's flaws are part of what make it sound great.

Glue-on vs. Bolt-on vs. Neck-thru-body

Some guitars have the neck glued to the body (Les Pauls), some are bolted on (Fenders), and in some the neck is part of one piece of wood that extends all the way through the body (Jackson). The theory of the neck-thru-body design is that, since the pick-ups and the bridge are mounted in the same piece of wood that makes up the neck, and the strings from tuners to tailpiece are on the same piece of wood, sustain will be greatly enhanced. In practice, a well joined glue-on or properly fitted bolt-on neck will sustain just as well as a neck-thru-body style. A neck-thru-body style does allow twenty-four frets without fear that the fingerboard will curl up—but on the downside, if anything goes irreparably wrong with the neck, the entire guitar is a total loss.

BODIES

Guitars come in all shapes and sizes, from the more traditonal arch-top, f-hole variety to exotic star shapes, to functional rail shapes that could hardly be said to have a body at all. The body of an electric guitar can affect the sound greatly or subtly. For example, there will be a great deal of difference between the sound of a big hollow bodied arch-top and a flying-V solid body, but a more subtle difference between an alder bodied strat and an ash one.

This Benedetto Cremona model archtop offers great tone at extremely low volume levels.

If you are going for a Wes Montgomery or Pat Metheney jazz tone, you will find it much more easily obtainable from a big body Gibson L-5 than from a Fender Telecaster. Keep in mind that like many of the suggestions in this book, this is just another suggestion, not a law engraved in stone. Jazz guitarists can be as susceptible to fashion as rock guitarists, and many of them play arch-tops as much because it is traditional and "cool" as for the warm tone. John Abercrombie, Mike Stern, and Ed Bickert all manage to get warm, beautiful tones out of solid body guitars. The more traditional players like Jim Hall and Joe Pass often play at volumes that lie somewhere between acoustic and electric, and thus prefer arch-tops which have more acoustic properties than solid bodies.

Semi-acoustic guitars, like the Gibson 335 and its many variations and imitators, offer advantages to the guitarist who plays both traditional jazz and rock. These guitars have a thinner hollow body than the big body archtops, and many have a solid piece of wood running up the middle of the body. The thin body offers only part of the acoustic resonance of the bigger body electrics, but this same lack of resonance allows them to be played at louder volumes without uncontrollable feedback. In this case, a solid block of wood running through the body does add sustain—something you may find lacking in bigger hollow bodies.

The main thing to keep in mind when choosing between hollow bodies and semi-hollow is that the features that give the guitar a good acoustic sound (thin top, solid wood top, f-holes, lots of air inside) are the same features that will cause it to feed back at relatively low volumes. You must decide what your playing requires to find the right compromise.

Solid bodies

The resonance of a solid body is much subtler than that of a hollow or semi-hollow body. Controversy still rages over the resonant qualities of various woods, but some basic information should help you decide what you need to achieve your sound.

A solid guitar body should be constructed out of no more than three pieces of wood. A one-piece body will probably resonate the best, but two and three piece bodies can sound quite good.

Ah, but what kind of wood? Different types of wood will have different sonic properties, but there are a few general rules to remember when trying to decide which wood is right for your sound.

First: Remember what I said about wood— no two pieces are identical. So while the sound of different types of wood will vary (ash, maple, alder), the sound of two bodies of the same type will vary as well, although more subtly.

Second: The body is only one component of a guitar, and therefore the sound of the body will be only one part of the total sound. For example, you may want to temper a dark sounding rosewood neck with a bright sounding maple body (or vice versa). Or, if your pickups sound a little harsh, you can use a warmer sounding body.

Third: While koa, zebrawood, and other exotic woods make lovely furniture, common sense would indicate that there must be a reason why virtually all of the world's most successful and distinctive guitarists have used guitars made of ordinary woods such as ash, alder, maple, and mahogany, even when they could afford more expensive woods. There *is* a reason—*sound.*

Over the years, orthodox theory about heavy versus light bodies has swung back and forth like a pendulum. Here again, your playing needs should determine your choice. The following may help you decide.

Certain heavier, denser woods (mahogany, heavy ash) sound fuller and sustain better than light woods at low volumes. When you crank up the volume, however, heavier bodies can muddy the sound. In these days of high decibel playing, the trend has been toward lighter bodies (swamp ash, alder, poplar). Lighter bodies resonate better and produce a clearer tone at high volumes. (They also can greatly reduce chiropractor bills!)

The shape of the body has a minimal effect on the tone. We all know that it is important to have a ''cool'' looking guitar, but keep in mind that if your only instrument is a Flying-V, you had better enjoy practicing standing up!

PICKS AND STRINGS

Many guitar players spend anywhere from hundreds to thousands of dollars in an attempt to get the sound that they hear in their head. They will buy new necks, new bodies, new pickups, or even new guitars and still feel that there is something lacking in their sound. They will eat peanut butter and jelly sandwiches every day for a month to be able to afford the latest electronic effect, when it is possible that they can solve their sonic problem for as little as twenty-five cents!

Picks

Try this—go into a music store and buy a thin pick, a medium pick, and a heavy pick of the same material (i.e. plastic, tortex, nylon). Choose the material and shape with which you are most comfortable (this may cost you anywhere from a quarter to a dollar). First, try playing your guitar acoustically with the light pick. Listen carefully to the tone. Now play the same notes and chords with the heavy pick. You will notice that the tone is much thinner and brighter with the light pick and thicker and darker with the heavy pick. Now try the medium. As you might suspect, the tone falls somewhere in between. You may have just saved yourself thousands of dollars and years of frustration.

Quite often, players are happy with the basic feel and tone of their instruments, but would still like the sound a little brighter. Changing from a heavy to a medium or light pick could give just the tonal change they are looking for. Conversely, if you are trying for a thicker tone and have been using a light gauge pick, you may have to switch

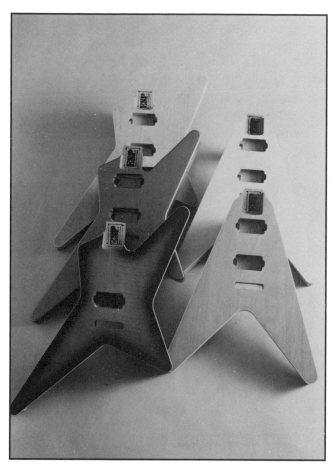

Wacky shapes won't necessarily add to the tone, but they will add to the fun!

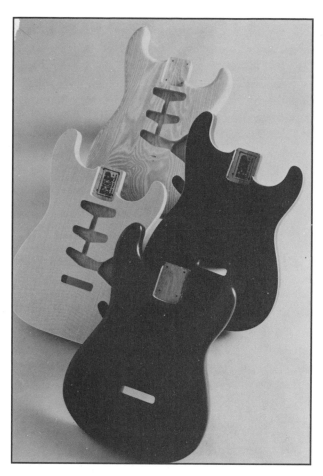

Replacement bodies are available in attractive woods that require only an oil finish, or perfectly suitable but less attractive woods that you may prefer painted.

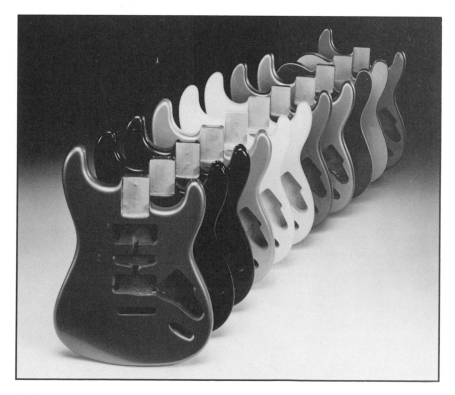

Bodies can be purchased in many exciting colors. Most are finished with acrylic paint. If you can afford it, having an unfinished body painted with nitrocellulose lacquer will allow the wood to breathe and will add to the tone.

to a heavier one. Changing pick gauge, may involve some modification of your picking technique, but the resulting sound could be well worth it.

Picks are now offered in a wide variety of materials—different plastics, nylon, graphite, tortex, stone, and metal. The type of material can affect the sound as much as the gauge and both will make as big a difference as a new set of pick-ups or a new body.

Strings

Strings are a somewhat larger investment than picks. You may have to spend as much as twenty or twenty-five dollars trying out different sets of strings until you find the right set for the sound that you want. But consider this scenario:

> *Customer: "I have an old Strat just like Stevie Ray Vaughn's and I know all his licks. I use the same amps and effects, I even wear the same clothes—why don't I sound like him?"*
> *Me: "Well, what gauge strings are you using?"*
> *Customer: ".008's."*
> *Me: "That could be your problem—Stevie uses .013's ."*

Strings, like picks, sound brighter and thinner in the lighter gauges, and thicker and darker in the heavier ones. If you are playing extremely loud music or with lots of distortion, the difference may not be very noticeable (though it is still discernable). However, at lower volumes or with a cleaner tone, the difference is much more pronounced.

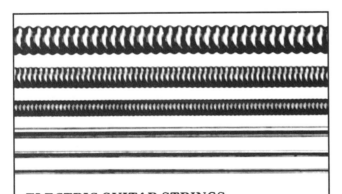

ELECTRIC GUITAR STRINGS
Reinforced for tremolos
Designed for tone
.009, .011, .016, .024, .032, .042
Made in U.S.A.

Strings come gauged in hundreths of an inch. It is a good idea to know your gauges, as one manufacturer's "light" is another's "extra - light."

In addition to different gauges, electric guitar strings come in different materials and styles. Most are made of nickel or stainless steel. These two materials each have their own sound, so try both and see which you like. Strings also come round-wound, flat-wound, and half-round. Most players use round-wound, but for less finger noise and a darker sound you may want to try the others.

In choosing the right gauge for your sound, you will have to decide what personal compromise you are willing to make between playability (lighter gauge) and tone (heavier gauge). But don't be afraid to work your way up by practicing on an acoustic guitar with heavier strings. When you return to playing the electric, you will find that you can move up a gauge or so.

Hint: Changes of string gauge may require a new set-up (see "set-ups").

Don't hesitate to move up or down one gauge according to circumstances. If you have not been playing for a few weeks, you can go to a lighter gauge temporarily (Jeff Beck does). What you lose in tone you will make up for in feeling comfortable, which is more important. You can also make up the tone with higher volume, or as Eddie Martinez (guitarist with Mick Jagger, Robert Palmer, etc.) says, "Using 009's? Just turn up!"

I wish I had a nickel for each time I have heard the complaint, "I'm not getting enough brightness out of my instrument" or "My guitar won't get/stay in tune," and I say, "When did you change your strings last?" only to be answered, "What year is this?"

Appropriate frequency of string changing depends on a number of factors:

1. Your body chemistry. Do you perspire when you play, and how corrosive is your sweat?
2. How long and how often do you play?
3. Do you live in a damp climate?
4. What brand of string do you use?

Depending on these factors, you may have to change your strings anywhere from every day to once a month. Corrosive sweat and damp climates will require that you change your strings more often than will dry hands and climates. If you play your guitar four to six hours a day, your strings will have to be changed more often than if you pick up your guitar once or twice a week. Also, some brands of strings wear out faster than others. You may, however, be willing to change these strings more often if you prefer their sound to longer-lasting ones.

Remember—The **sound** *is the thing!*

THE SETUP

It is hard to overemphasize the importance of a good setup. It can immeasurably improve the playability of any guitar, from the cheapest to the most expensive. Whether you are a beginner or an experienced player, I suggest you seek out a top notch repair person (preferably one who is a good player as well) to set up your guitar. It can cost anywhere from $20 to $40 or more for the best, but it is worth every penny and normally should not be needed more than three or four times per year, usually less. A setup should include:

Intonation—

For a guitar to play properly in tune, the distance from the nut to the twelfth fret should equal the distance from the twelfth fret to the place where the string crosses the bridge saddle. This distance is not the same for each string due to the variation in thickness from string to string. Intonation should be set only with new strings. A good repair person will be able to spot a bum string in a new set, but even the best cannot intonate a guitar with old strings.

The Nut—

We have already discussed the importance of the nut. A proper setup should include opening a nut that is too tight or shimming up a nut that is worn too low. Cutting a new nut usually costs extra.

Action—

This is the height of the strings over the fretboard. Be sure to indicate your preference to the person doing your setup *before* they start. **Note**—A higher action allows the strings to ring better and can result in improved tone. As with string gauges, you must find your own compromise between sound and playability.

Truss-rod adjustment—

The neck should be checked for bowing or back-bowing and the truss-rod adjusted to compensate.

Almost all new guitars require a setup. A proper setup should be tailored to you and your playing style. Even the most expensive guitars are initially set up for some average common denominator. The action must be adjusted to your preference and the nut cut for your choice of string gauge. These, in turn, will influence the intonation.

After you have owned the guitar for a while, periodic setups will be required with the change of seasons (depending on where you live) or when traveling with the instrument from one climate to another. Radical string gauge changes or action adjustments may also require a new setup. Trust your instincts—if the guitar doesn't play or sound quite right, bring it in for a check-up. Like a car, a good tune-up will make a big difference in how your guitar handles. On the other hand, don't feel that you must have it done at specific intervals—once again, the best rule of thumb is "If it ain't broke, don't fix it."

In the long run, it may be cheaper to have setups and other guitar work done by a skilled luthier—preferably one who is also a skilled player.

CHAPTER 2

The Electric Guitar as an Electric Instrument

THANKS TO THE ADVICE IN CHAPTER ONE, you are now the proud owner of an electric guitar with a great acoustic sound. The idea now is to amplify that sound so it can be heard over other instruments or simply by other people. The pickups, electronics, cable, and amplifier are all links in the chain of this amplification. In this chapter, I will explain how to make your guitar louder without sacrificing the sound quality we have achieved so far.

THE PICKUPS

The first link in the chain is the **pickup.** The pickup (or pickups, as the case may be) transfers a large amount of information to the amplifier. It must send the pitch, tone, volume, attack, and sustain characteristics of your guitar through the connecting cable to the input of your amp. Therefore, it is very important to choose carefully when deciding on the right pickup(s) for your sound. A very basic explanation of how an electric guitar pickup works will help you in making your decision.

A pickup is basically an electromagnet. Wire is wound around a permanent magnet (either solid or six pole pieces).When a guitar string vibrates through the magnet's field, an electrical current is sent through the wire and out to the am-

plifier. The bigger the magnet and the more windings of wire, the greater the output of the pickup. Therefore, the pickups with the biggest magnets and the most windings must be the best, right? *Wrong!!* As the number of windings increases, so does the power. Unfortunately, the high end frequency response drops. You will notice this if you try out some of your more heavy metal oriented pickups. In a clean mode there is a decided lack of treble response. In addition, big magnets will exert a pull on the strings, thus reducing sustain. It is for this reason that you should not raise either pickups or pole pieces too close to the strings.

Pickup magnets come in two types: **Alnico** (aluminum plus nickel plus cobalt added to iron) and **ceramic.** Ceramic magnets are cheaper to produce and provide more high end, but their high end tends to be somewhat brittle sounding. Alnico magnets have a warmer sound. Pickup manufacturers have been experimenting with various types of alnico magnets to try and achieve the sound of a vintage pickup. Some of this sound is due to the loss of magnetism over the years, so once again we see that power isn't everything.

Overwound pickups became popular in the days when the only way to achieve distortion was to have a pickup that was powerful enough to overdrive the amplifier. Their midrange heaviness was actually a plus when it came to making the tubes work beyond their capacity. Unfortunately, their clean sound left much to be desired.

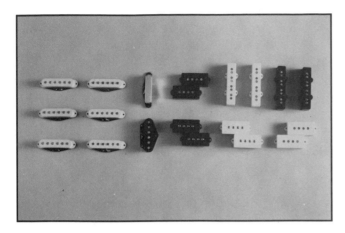

Left to right: Stratocaster pickups - single coil, Telecaster pickups - single coil, Precision bass pickups - humbucking, and far right top, Jazz bass pickups - single coil.

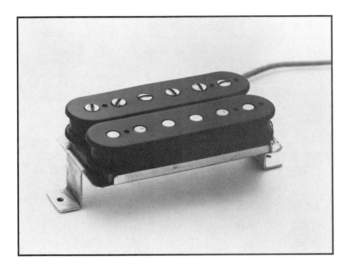

Double coil, humbucker pickup.

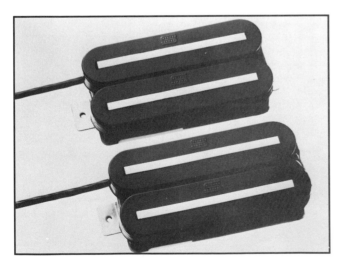

Double coil, humbucking pickup with rails instead of pole pieces. With this setup you needn't worry about your strings being positioned directly over the pole pieces. Theoretically, this will also minimize sustain loss as you bend the string away from its corresponding pole piece.

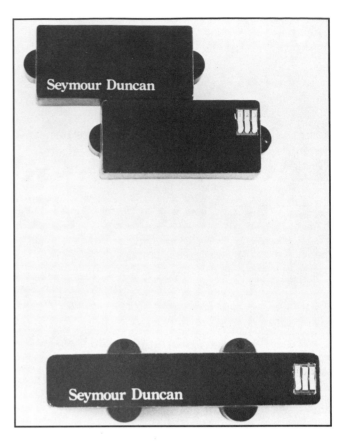

These active bass pickups have rocker switches to adjust their equalization.

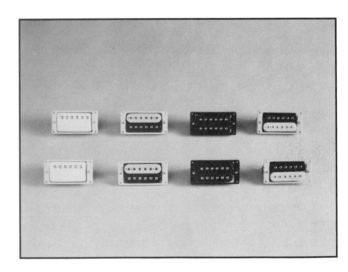

Humbucking pickups may be installed with or without metal covers. The tonal difference will be minimal, but if you decide on covers for aesthetic reasons, you should have the pickups dipped in wax or "potted" with the covers. This will minimize squealing feedback problems at high volume. Potting is recommended for single coil pickups as well, but they need not be dipped with their covers (if the covers are plastic).

Since the start of the fabulous eighties, we have seen a glut of amplifiers with built-in overdrive, not to mention a multitude of overdrive, distortion, and heavy metal pedals. These scientific wonders have eliminated the need for overwound pickups because it is no longer necessary for the pickup to overdrive the amplifier. Today's desirable pickup must strike a balance between having enough gain to properly drive effects, but few enough windings to maximize high end response.

There are two basic types of pickup: **single-coil** and **double-coil.** A single-coil pickup is just one set of windings around one bobbin (usually made of plastic) containing the magnet(s). A double-coil pickup is usually (but not always, as we shall see later) two single-coil pickups side-by-side. The two coils are wired together in series (one into the next, which increases their power) and electronically out of phase. Wiring them out of phase eliminates the hum that is normally picked up by single coil pickups from lighting sources, room wiring and amplifier transformers (which is why moving away from the amp can reduce hum from a single coil pickup). This hum-cancelling effect is what gave rise to the name "humbuckers" for double-coil pickups. These days that name can be misleading, as there are many pickups available that look and sound like single-coils, but are in fact "hum-bucking." Some of these single-coil sounding pickups are actually two coils stacked one on top of the other instead of side by side. This allows them to fit in a single coil route on a guitar while effectively cancelling the hum.

Confused? You should be. However, it is best thought of like this. When choosing a pickup, your first concern should be *sound*. Does it have enough power for your needs without sacrificing the high end that you want? Does it have the *sound* you want? If this sound requires a vintage single-coil pickup or a current replacement, don't worry too much if it hums. Jeff Beck, Ritchie Blackmore, Mark Knopfler, and Eric Clapton have performed and recorded for years with single-coil pickups and all of their inherent noise. I don't know of one case in which a fan of these musicians returned records or requested a refund after a live show because of "hum."

If single coil pickups just don't have enough "punch" for you and you need a little more power, you may be a candidate for a double-coil, or "humbucking," pickup. It is important that you specify a side-by-side double-coil because part of the sound that is associated with this type of pickup is a result of the coils picking up sound from two different points on the string length. This gives a fuller sound than is possible with a single-coil. Unfortunately, this also results in a phase cancellation that, along with the extra windings inherent in twice as many coils, reduces the high end available. Once again you must decide on a compromise that best suits your style. Later on, we will cover wiring tricks and effects at your disposal that can make a single-coil sound like a double-coil (and vice versa).

You may want to consider the advantages of **active pickups.** These are pickups that use a battery for power. Active pickups are extremely quiet and can be very powerful without sacrificing any high end. They do not have to be grounded to the strings (passive pickups ordinarily do), thereby eliminating the possibility of electric shock when you grab the microphone and the strings simultaneously. Studio engineers love active pickups because they compress a wide tonal range into a limited volume range. This means they can get a lot of treble and bass respone without distorting the tape. Unfortunately, this compression effect limits the variety of attack possible with active pickups. Since much of the personality in your sound is put there by the way you attack the strings, active pickups can tend to make everyone sound alike (more about this under "compressors"). This is not necessarily a problem if you want to be a studio guitarist. However, if you are trying to develop a distinctive sound of your own, you may find that this disadvantage outweighs all the other advantages. Manufacturers claim that the newer 18 volt active systems eliminate this compression effect. Try them and judge for yourself.

Another important factor in choosing the right pickup is its location on the guitar. Although they are often labelled as such, there is actually no tonal difference between a bridge pickup, a middle pickup, and a neck pickup. When a pickup is recommended for the bridge position, it only means that it is wound a little hotter than one of the same type or model that is recommended for the neck or middle position. This is because the strings put out less volume near the bridge than near the neck or middle. So, to balance the pickups when they are used simultaneously, the bridge pickup should have more output than the neck or middle ones.

The difference in tone achieved by your pickups is due almost entirely to their location. Play the guitar acoustically. Pick near the bridge, near the neck, near the middle. You will hear a trebly sound near the bridge which gets warmer and less trebly as you approach the neck. All that the pickups do is "pick up" this sound. The identical pickup, moved from bridge to middle to neck on the guitar, will provide three extremely different sounds.

This location business becomes very important when discussing the much sought after, so-called "out-of-phase" sound. This sound, popularized by Mark Knopfler and Eric Clapton, has nothing to do with Stratocasters, electronic phasing, or type of pickup. It has everything to do with *location* of the pickups and the balance between them.

The sound in question is produced by string phasing—hence the confusion. When a guitar string vibrates, it creates a wave-like pattern. While one pickup is transmitting one part of the wave, the adjacent pickup is transmitting another part. Without getting too technical, suffice to say that the distance between the bridge pickup and the middle pickup of a Stratocaster creates a unique phase cancellation that results in that *"Dire Straits"* type of tone that we know and love. (A similar but less trebly tone results when the middle and neck pickup are on.)

It is not necessary to have a Stratocaster-type guitar or even single-coil pickups to achieve this tone. Two double-coil humbuckers can achieve the same effect. However, it *is* necessary that the pickups be spaced similarly to the Stratocaster bridge and middle or neck and middle pickups. A bridge and neck pickup used simultaneously will never result in that particular tone, no matter what fancy wiring or equalization you attempt. However, many Telecaster owners have had great success by putting a Stratocaster pickup in between their two existing pickups and installing a five-way switch. It is also necessary that the pickups be balanced properly. If one overpowers the other, the sound will lack that familiar "funkiness."

Try not to be discouraged by the enormous number of pickup makes and models available. Once you understand the principles explained above, you should be able to ask enough intelligent questions so that an informed salesman will be able put you on the right track. However, there is no escaping the bottom line—*you don't know how the pickup is going to sound in your set-up until you actually put it in your guitar.* Since pickup prices range from $30-$100, experimenting can be expensive. Fortunately, some pickup manufacturers, like Seymour Duncan, realize this. If you purchase one of their pickups and it doesn't sound right for your purposes, they will offer to exchange it (usually within twenty or thirty days of purchase) for another model of equal value. You may have to sell or trade other manufacturers' pickups to defray the cost of experimentation.

It is important that you find the right pickups to go with your guitar. The guitar must sound good going straight into the amplifier before we start adding any effects.

WIRING SYSTEMS

In addition to which pickup you choose, how that pickup is wired within itself and in conjunction with other pickups will greatly affect the tone coming out.

Within the Pickup

Coil-tapping is more often applied to single rather than double-coil pickups. It involves tapping a second output part way through the windings of the pickup. A switch is installed to allow you to go from full output to the tapped output. This wiring is employed when using overwound single coil pickups of the "quarter-pounder" variety. It allows you to get more high end in the tapped position because you have temporarily reduced the number of windings employed in the pickup.

Many double-coil humbucker owners would like to be able to get a single coil type sound out of these pickups. The most common method employed is *coil-splitting.* This involves installing a switch that allows them to ground out one of the two coils in the pickup, leaving them with a single-coil pickup of sorts. There are two major drawbacks to this system: 1) *They now have all the hum and single-coil noise inherent in a single-coil pickup.* If they are normally using this humbucking pickup together with one or two single-coil "stacks," it will now add noise to an otherwise noiseless system. 2) *If they are employing a moderately powerful humbucker, each coil in it is much less powerful than the average single-coil pickup.* This means that in single-coil mode, this pickup will sound weak and thin by itself and will not balance properly with true single-coil pickups. Remember that balance is vital to achieve that two-pickup "Strat" tone.

An alternative to coil-splitting is *series-parallel* wiring. Remember I said that the two coils in a side-by-side humbucker are normally wired in series? Well, by installing a switch that changes this wiring to parallel, you can change the sound of the pickup without losing the hum cancelling properties. The output will be reduced to almost single-coil level, and the tone will show an increase in high end. This wiring will still not provide sound and output identical with that of a single-coil pickup, but at least you will not add any noise.

Our next wiring possibility falls somewhere in between internal and external wiring. This involves taking two "Strat" type single-coil pickups and wiring them together, in series, right next to each other in the guitar. If you use two stacks, you can then split them and have a true single-coil sound with no hum. If you don't use stacks, be sure one of the singles is reverse-wrap, reverse polarity from the other. Otherwise, when they are on simultaneously in series, they will be too noisy. Together, these two pickups will provide very close to a true humbucker sound, and when split, you will have a real single-coil.

External

Once you have chosen your pickup or pickups, they must be wired together and then wired to whatever volume and tone controls you desire. Multiple pickups are normally wired in parallel. You may want to have the option of switching to series. Brian May of the group *Queen* gets a very distinctive tone by wiring his single coil pickups together in series. Keep in mind, however, that this can increase noise and reduce high end.

You have your choice of three-way, five-way, or individual switches for your pickups, and you can add as many mini-switches, push-pull pots, or other switching devices as you need to achieve all of the pickup combinations you desire.

You will also need to control the volume from your guitar. You may want individual volumes for each pickup, but it is a good idea to have a master volume located where you can easily reach it. (Turning down the overall volume on a Les Paul without changing the tone can be very tricky when you are using both pickups.) If your tone changes radically as you turn down your volume, this can be fixed by the judicious use of capacitors by you or your repair person.

Tone controls can be either *active* or *passive*. Passive tone controls are, in effect, volume controls for tone. The same electronic part that is used for volume controls is used in tone controls. A capacitor is added to it that tells it to lower only the volume of a certain frequency. In most guitars this frequency is treble, but there are other possibilities. There are "tone-cubes" that filter out mid-range or bass, as well as vary-tone switches available. These offer a five or six-position switch with a different capacitor for each position. The use of any of these types of tone controls will lower the overall volume of the instrument. You will find, however, that even though the actual output of the guitar is lower, certain capacitors will give a much fuller tone and will make the sound appear louder.

Active tone controls use a little battery-powered preamp to add treble, mid-range, or bass, and will increase the volume of the guitar. Some players find this tone a little harsh—try a guitar with active tone controls and judge for yourself.

One solution for the guitarist who likes the sound of single-coil pickups, but who would like more power is the *on-board pre-amp*—a little amplifier built right into the guitar. It will increase the volume without adversely affecting the tone. In fact, it will help restore the high end lost traveling down the cable and through the effects. In addition, there are tone-cubes available for use in conjunction with these preamps. For example, a preamp used together with a mid-range cube can allow you to instantly increase both the power and mids of a single-coil pickup—turning it into an instant humbucker! Before installing one of these miracle workers into your guitar, you should know that they also boost any noise in the instrument. Be sure your pickups are quiet and that the guitar is well shielded and grounded first.

Hint: Feel free to load your instrument with all the "gimcracks" and "geegaws" you like. But, before you end up with a guitar that looks like the instrument panel on the Concorde, you may want to think about where you will be using it. If it is in the studio, the more the merrier. Odds are that you will be able to tune in the exact sound you need for the track and play it straight through. You will then have time to reset all of your dials and switches for the next track.

If, however, you will most often be playing your instrument live, you should probably keep it simple. You may be required to go from one sound to another rapidly while singing and/or dancing. If that is the case, you will not want to have to reset three switches and turn two knobs to get from one sound to another. When playing in most live situations, many subtleties of tone are lost, so you will find that a simple setup will provide you with all the tonal variation you need. Besides, there are still plenty of outboard sound modifiers to come which can be operated by foot, leaving your hands free to play.

THE AMPLIFIER

You could say that the amplifier is not technically part of the guitar, but in the case of an electric instrument, for all intents and purposes, it is. After all, imagine trying to play in a band, or even a large room by yourself, without an amplifier. In the past there have even been electric guitars with built-in amps (remember the Telecaster with the speaker under the strings?). So it would appear that the amplifier is actually a sort of modular part of the instrument itself. Its job is to take the sound being produced by the guitar and make it audible (or deafening, if that is your particular bent).

But which amplifier? This brings up all sorts of confusing questions—should I buy a solid state amp? Tube amp? Separate preamp and power amp?

Once again, these questions involve personal taste, but the confusion can be lessened by the understanding of a few basic principles.

A word about how they work

Guitar amplifiers consist of two stages—the *preamp* and the *power amp*. The function of the preamp is to raise the power of the signal coming from the pickups to a level that will drive the power amp. The power amp stage then gives you enough level to drive the speakers and to be heard at the back of the room (or the next county). That is probably all the technical information you need to known how to get a good sound.

The first two questions you need to ask yourself when choosing an amplifier are: "What kind of music am I going to play?" and "Where am I going to play it?" You may choose to use a different amp for playing country music in a small bar than you would for playing heavy metal in a coliseum—although we shall see that the same amp could theoretically be used for both.

An amplifier tends to sound best when it is being pushed. Even if you are seeking a clean tone, it will sound fullest at the point just before distortion. And, as we shall see in the next section, the best distortion comes from overdriving the power stage of a tube amplifier.

To determine how much wattage you need, you must decide how loud your clean sound needs to be. If you need to play clean Metheney-esque solos over the entire band, or thin, funky, James Brown type rhythm work that will cut through a horn section, you will need a powerful amplifier. A transistor amp will usually deliver more clean power than a tube amp of the same wattage (hence

the popularity of the Roland JC 120). However, many players find the sound of a transistor amp harsh and brittle.

These days, high powered p.a. systems are often available to further amplify your amplifier. In this case, your main considerations should be how loud the drummer plays and how far away from your amp you intend to be. As long as your amplifier can give you a clean sound that you can hear over the drummer at the farthest distance you need to go, it is powerful enough. Soundmen prefer that you do not throw too much sound off of the stage, but rather that the sound come through the p.a. where they can control it. At first this may seem unnatural, but if you can become comfortable with it, your band will sound much better. Keep in mind that the vocal mikes are picking up your amplifier as well.

If you must turn your amplifier up to distortion levels in order to hear yourself, but what you want is a clean sound, then you may need more power—or, the rest of the band may be too loud. Remember, this isn't a contest—guide yourself by the drums. The drummer should play at a comfortable level for the style of music, and the rest of the band should arrange their volume around the drums.

If distortion is your style, you should still guide yourself by the drums. As we shall see in the next chapter, there are different degrees of distortion. If you are overdriving your amp to get a distorted sound, you will only get a great sound within a very limited volume range. If you are forced to turn up your amp too far or not far enough, you will not achieve the desired sound. So, it is important that the amplifier is not over or underpowered for the situation.

Do not be deceived by famous bands that appear to be using row upon row of hundred watt amplifiers. There is a method to this madness—in some cases, it is pure show business.

Some friends of mine were once the opening act for the hard rock group *Heart*. *Heart* performed in front of a wall of speaker cabinets stacked fifteen feet high. Their sound was loud, but perfectly controlled. My friend informed me that the guitarist was using only one Twin-Reverb that was miked behind that wall of speakers. The speaker cabinets were all empty! They served as a kind of stage set.

In some cases, when you see a wall of speakers stretching across a large stage, it is so the guitarist can hear his or her sound at any point onstage. But when you see six Marshall heads for each guitarist, it is highly doubtful that all are in

This Seymour Duncan 60 Watt Convertible amplifier allows you to switch from a clean channel to a distorted channel.

This 100 watt version of the Duncan amp offers separate amounts of reverb and different equalization for each channel. Seymour Duncan amps also offer changeable preamp modules to vary the overall sound of the amplifier.

use (or even plugged in). This is more likely because, in addition to the showbiz value, Marshall heads being pushed into distortion night after night have a dismaying tendency to blow up. Six heads allow the roadie to plug in a new one each time one gives up. One, or at most two, one hundred watt heads should supply more than enough power for even the largest stage and the loudest drummer.

I would rather not get involved in the tube vs. transistor battle. I have mentioned the loudness vs. wattage factor, but you should also be aware that transistor amps are usually smaller and lighter than tube amps. There are also hybrids—transistor preamps combined with tube power amps and vice versa. My personal preference is for the warmth of tubes, but great sounds can be obtained from either. Try them both and decide for yourself.

SPEAKERS

Guitar amplifiers may have one or more speakers contained in the same cabinet as the power and preamps, or they may be contained in separate cabinets. When talking about speakers, one usually is interested in "efficiency," or how efficiently the speaker translates the power put out by the amplifier into sound. A fifty watt amplifer will sound louder when plugged into more efficient speakers . For example—a Marshall head will sound louder plugged into a cabinet loaded with four 12″ Electrovoice speakers than on the same settings plugged into four 12″ Celestion speakers wired identically. This is because Electrovoice speakers are more efficient than Celestions. However, Celestions have a certain tone that is preferred for a particular type of rock sound. As we saw in the section on pickups—loudness is not everything.

Another consideration when discussing speakers is "resistance," which is measured in "ohms." Individual speakers are usually four, eight, or sixteen ohms. The higher the number, the more resistance. The speaker output on the back of your amplifier should indicate the recommended speaker resistance for maximum efficiency. You may plug into a cabinet offering *more* resistance (you just won't get as much volume), **but never plug into a cabinet offering less resistance than is recommended.** If you do, you risk blowing up the amplifier. Keeping this in mind, you may want to experiment with plugging your amplifier head

into various speaker types and configurations (one 12″ speaker, two 12″ speakers, two 10″ speakers, four 12″ speakers, etc.).

For some of you, this is all you need—a great sounding guitar plugged into a great sounding amplifier. In an ideal performing and recording world, this would be all any of us would need—all other effects would be added at the p.a. or mixing board. But what are these effects and what do they do? And, in this less-than-perfect world, how do you control them yourself in order to keep less-than-competent soundpersons and recording engineers from wreaking havoc with your dulcet tones?

How indeed? Read on!

PART
TWO

The Effects

CHAPTER 3
Distortion and Sustain

GUITARISTS HAVE BEEN JEALOUS of the superior volume and sustain available to other instrumentalists ever since the guitar was invented. Horns were louder and could hold a note until the player's breath ran out (or with circular breathing, indefinitely). The church organ sustained as long as the key was pressed and was capable of majestic volume. Even the less powerful violins and other strings could hold a note until the player's bowing arm got tired. The invention of electric guitars and amplifiers instantly solved the volume problem, but guitarists remained envious of the sustain capabilities of horns and organs.

There are two different, apocryphal stories concerning the discovery of distortion. One has it that a tube came loose in an amplifier, creating a distorted sound. The other is that a speaker was torn. It is unlikely that either case would create a sound that guitarists would covet. It is far more likely that one day a guitarist decided to go for broke, turning up one of those early, fifteen watt amplifiers until it started to overload the tubes. This would cause the tubes to distort and create a warm, singing tone somewhat resembling that of a saxophone. *Eureka!*

In addition to the resemblence in tone, the lucky guitarist found that his notes sustained longer—not as long as a horn, but long enough to alter the way guitarists would phrase their lines from that point forward.

This sustain was caused by the "compression" effect of tubes distorting—which brings us to the first of the "effects"!

COMPRESSION

To understand the use of compression and compressors, we must first understand the difference between *distortion* and *sustain*. Distortion is a description of a type of sound. The ear hears certain overtones around the note that it discerns as distortion (more on this in the next section). Sustain refers to how long the note remains audible. Distortion can sometimes increase sustain, but sustain can also be increased without any distortion.

We discussed how to maximize the acoustic sustain of your guitar in the first section. This is very important because no electric device will make up for choking strings or poorly cut nuts. However, once your guitar is sustaining nicely acoustically, a compressor can increase the "apparent" sustain of your instrument. As you read on, you will understand why I say "apparent," and why the natural sustain of the instrument is so important.

How compression works

It is easiest to understand compressors if you think of them as "automatic volume pedals." No matter how hard or how soft you strike the strings, the compressor reduces the volume sent to the amplifier to a pre-set level. Then, as the string slows its vibrations and the volume sent by the pickup(s) drops, a little amplifier in the compressor gradually raises the volume to keep it at the same level as the initial attack.

You can see how this works for yourself. Plug in your guitar and stand next to your amplifier. Set it for a clean sound. Now strike a note—and as the volume drops, keep turning up your amplifier volume. You will hear that the note appears to be sustaining longer. You will understand why I say "appears" if you try it again without turning up the volume. Listen closely. Now try it the first way again. You will hear that the actual note does not last any longer when you turn up the volume, it just remains louder longer. If it is still unclear, see Figure 3.

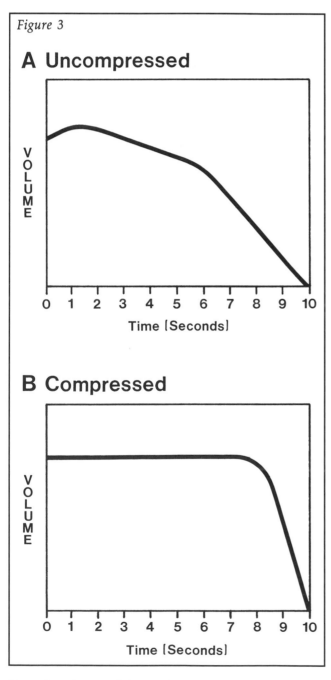

Figure 3

A Uncompressed

VOLUME

Time (Seconds)

B Compressed

VOLUME

Time (Seconds)

Note that the sound doesn't last any longer—it just stays louder longer.

Apparent or not, this extra sustain can come in handy. Compressors have many applications in getting great sounds. Adrian Belew has one "on," with the sustain at maximum at all times. When he plays his clean rhythms, you can hear the "squeezing" effect of the dampened attack. At the same time, the sustain makes his chorusing and flanging effects that much more dramatic. The incredible, highly controlled feedback that he gets is a combination of compression and distortion, but you will find that if you play around with a compressor, you can often get controlled feedback with virtually no distortion.

Andy Summers, of the former group *Police*, used compression combined with mild flanging to achieve the distinctive chiming sound on their records.

Another use for compressors is to even out the sound produced by the guitar. Even the best made guitars will have some notes that sound louder than others. A compressor will lower the sound of the loud notes and raise the volume of the quieter ones. It can also make up for defects in your technique. A note that is struck tentatively will come out just as strong as one struck forcefully, making your playing sound more confident than, perhaps, it is. Acoustic guitars are often compressed so that the bass strings do not overpower the treble ones.

Compression is often used in the studio to keep from overloading the tape or to help certain instruments stand out in the mix. Other effects, such as octavers, function better when receiving the consistent signal provided by a compressor.

Of course, there is a down side. As I mentioned when discussing active pickups, compression limits your dynamics and attack (some types of compressors are actually called "limiters"). Since much of the distinctiveness of your playing style is contained in the way you attack the strings and the dynamics of your playing, compression tends to homogenize your sound. Adrian Belew and Andy Summers are identifiable more for their concept and use of effects than their touch, but players like Larry Carlton, Robben Ford, Albert King and Mark Knopfler would be ill-served by excessive compression.

Keep in mind that compression is not an all or nothing proposition. Most compressors have two or three knobs. One should be marked "volume" or "output." This knob allows you to adjust the overall gain coming out of the unit. You can make your volume louder, softer, or identical when the unit is switched on. By increasing this gain, you can use the compressor as a preamp—a little increase will make up for gain that is lost running through subsequent cables and effects, and a big increase can be used to overdrive your amp.

Another knob will be "sustain," "compression," or "effect." This will determine how intense an effect you will create. Remember—there is a trade-off between sustain and dynamics.

Some compressors have an attack knob. This lets you regulate how much your initial attack is "squeezed" independent of the sustain.

I have found that compressors are usually more appropriate in a low-to-moderate volume situation. At higher volumes, the natural compression of the amplifier (especially tube amps) will provide sufficient sustain.

Warning: Compressors do not differentiate between music and noise. If you leave your compressor on and are not playing a note, it will try to raise the level of the noise coming through. For this reason, it is best to bypass it when not actually playing.

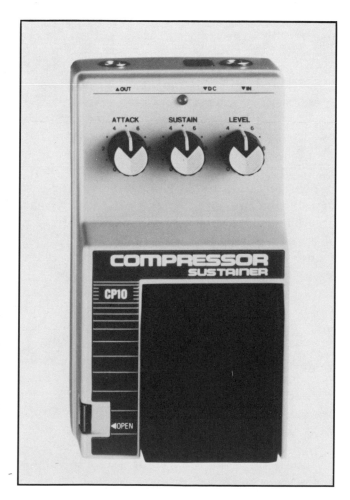

Some floor pedal compressors have an "attack" knob.

DISTORTION

For some, rock guitar is not rock guitar without distortion. It is true that ever since Chuck Berry's classic solo on "Maybelline," and probably even before, rock guitarists have been distorting the sound of their instruments. The sound of an amplifier driven to its limits and beyond is, to a great extent, the basic sound of rock and roll. *But what is distortion?*

Amplifiers were initially developed to take a weak signal and make it louder without changing its character. But when amplifiers receive too powerful a signal, the character of the signal changes. This change is what we hear as distortion. When a guitar with a very powerful pickup is turned all the way up, it can send out a signal that is too powerful for the amplifier—thus causing distortion.

Overloaded tubes create what is called "soft" distortion. Overloaded transistors create "hard" distortion. Transistors tend to remain clean up to a certain point and then distort, whereas tubes move more gradually from clean into increasing amounts of distortion. This gives tube distortion greater dynamic possibilities.

Soft distortion is often heard in nature. A bird singing, a whistle blowing, a saxophone—all are examples of soft distortion. This is why tube distortion is generally considered more "natural" than the transistor type.

Back to history for a moment. Early guitar amplifiers used tubes and were of relatively low wattage (10 to 20 watts). Early pickups, such as the Gibson P-90 , were quite powerful. It was easy for early rock guitarists to distort their amplifiers at relatively low volumes ("relative" to the present day—at the time, they were considered offensively loud!).

The beginnings of modern rock guitar sound can be traced back to one man, and even one album! "Bluesbreakers - John Mayall - Eric Clapton" featured a young guitarist who had just left a successful English pop band. Eric Clapton had garnered a reputation while with the *Yardbirds* that was built more on speed than on tone. He had even earned the ironic nickname "Slowhand." But it was with John Mayall's *Bluesbreakers* that he recorded the album that set a standard for rock guitar tone, a standard that is still studied to this day—ask Eddie Van Halen!

How did Clapton get the tone that started the expression "Clapton is God"? He played an early flame-topped Gibson Les Paul through a 50 watt Marshall combo amplifier with two twelve-inch speakers. And he played very loudly. And when the engineer asked him to turn down because the amplifier was distorting, *he said no!*

To this day, this remains the best sounding distortion that money can buy—the power tubes of a tube amp overdriven by a hot guitar. Note that I say "power tubes." As a rule, distorting the preamp tubes will not give as desirable a sound, which is why master volumes are not the answer. Some allow you to distort the pre-amp tubes while reducing the signal to the power tubes, which tends to produce a thinner tone than distorting the power tubes. Others involve splitting the power tube in half—better, but still not ideal.

But you may ask, " How can I get this sound without (a) losing my hearing, (b) getting fired by the Holiday Inn manager (who wants the latest Van Halen single played at conversational levels), or (c) blowing up my amplifier?" "There is more than one way to skin a cat," I answer.

One solution is an *attenuator.* This is basically just a big volume knob that goes between your amplifier and your speakers. It allows you to turn up your amplifier until it gives you the desired distortion, and then turn down the output to the speakers until you achieve the desired volume. The advantage of this method is that you are overdriving the power tubes which will give you the desirable overtones. The disadvantages are that (a) you are overdriving the power tubes continuously, causing them to wear out frequently(and they are expensive to replace), (b) you may wear out the transformer (which is even more expensive to replace), and (c) you can not get a very loud, clean sound should you need one.

Another solution is to use a smaller amp. Jimmy Page recorded the first few *Led Zeppelin* albums with a Telecaster through a small Silvertone amp turned up loud. In the studio, a small amp can sound very big. Even in a live situation, with today's p.a.'s, a properly miked small amp can sound as big as a Marshall stack. Jeff Baxter, of the *Doobie Brothers*, used to play stadiums using only a Fender Deluxe Reverb (15 or 20 watts) facing him as a monitor and miked through a 1,000 watt p.a....

Unfortunately, this does not solve either problem (c), nor does it solve another problem that arose as technology made more and more former studio effects available for stage use. When amplifier distortion is used in conjuction with a stage full of choruses, flangers, and delays, the distortion starts to sound muddy, dull, and unpleasant. That "Clapton is God" tone becomes adulterated. This is not a problem in the studio because the distorted sound is processed after the fact—that is, a clean signal is sent to the amplifier where it is distorted. That sound is then picked up by the microphone and put through other processing devices at the board. In a live situation where amplifier distortion is used, the clean signal is processed by choruses and/or delays, and that processed signal is then distorted by the amp. I will go into this more deeply in Chapter Five. Suffice to say for now that it is more desirable that the distortion come first. When this problem and all of the others mentioned above were tackled by technicians, their answer was the *distortion box.*

Early distortion boxes sounded not at all like an overdriven tube amplifier. They were aptly dubbed "fuzztones" due to their buzzsaw-like tone. Listen to Jeff Beck with the *Yardbirds* or Jimi Hendrix albums for examples of this sound. These two wizards of the electric guitar managed to extract highly musical sounds from these crude electronic devices. More recent years have seen Adrian Belew produce synthesizer, cello, and even animal sounds from semi-antique fuzz boxes. Though some players like these units for their unique tone or to evoke the psychedelic sixties, the majority of guitarists seek a box that will best imitate the sound of an overdriven amp.

Over the years, technology has made great strides in simulating the sound of overdriven tubes through the use of transistors and other non-tube technology. Current distortion devices have a much warmer, more natural tone than in years gone by.

"But why not just use tubes?" I hear you asking. Good question. It would seem to be the obvious solution. Until recently, however, no one has been able to come up with a distortion device that successfully used tube technology. Using power tubes necessitated too large a box, and using a preamp tube presented the same sound problem as with master volumes.

Fortunately, in recent years a solution has been found whereby a preamp tube can be put in a small box and be made to sound like power tubes overdriving. This allows today's guitarists to have all of the overtones and dynamics of tube distortion without (a) having to play at deafening volumes, (b) blowing up their amp, or (c) giving up their high volume clean sound.

It is interesting that one part of the solution that allowed the development of this type of distortion device was the use of equalization—interesting because it illustrates what an important role equalization, or "e.q.," plays in getting a good distorted tone. You can see this for yourself by setting up your amp or your distortion box for a mod-

If you wish to distort your amplifier but your pickups are not powerful enough, you may find that a preamp is the answer.

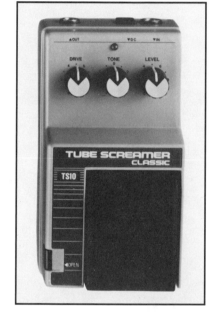

Programmable devices allow you to select any number of different distortion sounds at the flick of a switch.

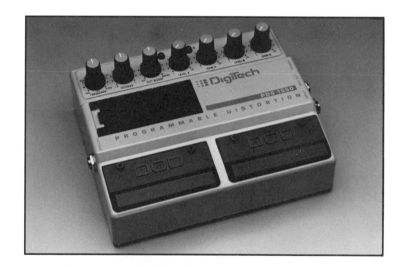

Technology has managed to come extremely close to approximating the sound of overdriven tubes.

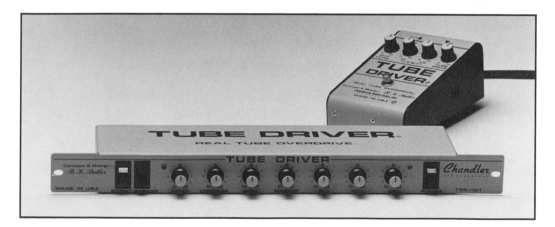

The best way to get the sound of an overdriven tube is still to use a tube. Proper equalization allows this device to make a 12AX7 preamp tube sound like an overdriven quartet of 6V6 or 6550 power tubes.

erate amount of distortion, and then playing with the tone controls on the amp and the guitar. You will notice a distinct change in the type of distortion you achieve as you change the tone of your amp and instrument.

Most distortion devices now come with tone controls as part of the package. Also, most channel-switching amps come with (or should come with) separate tone controls for the clean and distorted channels. This allows you to set up a bright, thin, funky sound for your clean sound, and a mid-range heavy, fat sound for your distortion. If your distortion box does not have any tone controls, or your amp has only one set for both channels, you will be forced to compromise. This usually results in being more or less dissatisfied with both sounds.

One of the most common problems that today's guitarists have with distortion is not too little, but too much. They use it to cover a multitude of sins—poor tone, poor sustain, and poor technique! Thus, I offer this advice for the first of many times throughout this book: *When it comes to effects, use only as much or as many as you need!*

Too much distortion will muddy and "fuzz up" your sound. If you are playing fast, it will make the notes blur into one another and, in general, will make your sound sink back in the overall mix.

If your lead tone is thin, try working with e.q. or some of the suggestions in Part One (heavier strings, heavier pick, better sounding pickups, etc.) *before* turning up the distortion. If you are lacking sustain, go over Part One and/or try adding a compressor rather than adding more fuzz.

Work on other aspects of your sound and technique and you may be suprised at how little distortion you need to get a good lead tone. Tube amps or distortion devices will distort more if you attack the strings harder. By adjusting the level of distortion and working on your technique, you can control the amount of distortion by how hard you play.

For a number of years, I played clubs in a band with another guitarist. We used comparable sized and powered amps, but the other guitarist favored double-coil pickups and a distortion box, whereas I played single coil-pickups and used a compressor to slightly overdrive my amp and add sustain. When playing without the band, his tone sounded fat and musical, whereas mine was thinner and slightly harsh. However, when we played in a band context, people commented (and tapes confirmed) that his solos were buried and lost and mine rang through.

There are a number of lessons to be learned from this, the most obvious being that sometimes "less is more." Also, we learn that sometimes what sounds good playing by ourselves will not work in a band context. So keep in mind that, even if heavy metal is your medium, try not to overdo the distortion.

Over the years you may find yourself using any or all of the types of distortion mentioned above. Try experimenting with each of them so that you will be able to get the sound you want in any context.

CHAPTER 4
Ambient Effects

CONSIDER THE FOLLOWING SITUATION: It is 5:30 pm on Friday. The band sets up its equipment at the club, and the musicians set their levels for typical playing volume. The drummer counts off a tune and the band begins their soundcheck. The roar is deafening; all of the instruments merge together into a reverberating wall of mush! Everyone cuts back the volume and, while this is easier on the ears, it does little to improve the sound. The band goes to dinner and hopes for the best.

Later that evening, the band returns to a sold-out show—people are hanging from the rafters! The band launches into the first tune only to find that their instruments sound so quiet and separate from one another that they must double their volume on the second tune just to make it sound like music.

The situation I have just described happens all the time. The odds are that if you are in a band, or know one well enough to attend their soundchecks, you have observed it yourself. What we have here is an example of the *ambience* of a room changing from sound check to gig time.

What is *ambience*? You may have heard the word used in referring to a restaurant. In that case, it refers to the ''atmosphere'' of the place, or literally, ''the surrounding air.'' When discussing sound, we are not discussing sound in a vacuum, we are discussing sound in the air around it. For the most part, we are also discussing the walls, floor, and ceiling around the air (we will leave headphones and open air concerts out for now).

When the band described previously was doing its soundcheck, the sound was bouncing off the hardwood stage and dance floor, the mirrored walls and concrete ceiling, blending into a muddy wall of noise. When the club filled up with people for the show, those people's bodies and clothing absorbed the sound coming off the stage until each instrument sounded totally separate from the others. They absorbed so much of the sound that the band was forced to raise its volume to fill the room.

Every room you play in will have a different ambience. The same room will have a different ambience from minute to minute, depending upon the number of people in it! A standing joke in one of my bands was that the sound of a room could change just because a guy named Fred walked in. This is not as off-the-wall as it seems. When playing the same room, five sets a night, six nights a week for six weeks, using the same equipment, playing the same tunes, you tend to notice the slightest variations in sound. A humid night can drastically alter the ambience of a room. Since sound travels through air, the thickness of that air and its water content will have an effect on the sound.

Up until the last thirty or forty years, music was always played or recorded in rooms built or chosen for their pleasing acoustic properties. In more recent decades, this has not always been the case. The explosion of ''popular'' music (as opposed to church or classical music) has forced musicians to play in clubs that are less than acoustically ideal (as opposed to churches and specially designed concert halls). Fortunately, at the same time modern recording techniques have required studio engineers to invent ways of modifying the ambience artificially.

Early recording engineers would place the musicians in an acoustically good room and put up one or two microphones to record them as if an audience were listening. Some great sounding early recordings were made this way (check out early Duke Ellington records or Archie Bell and the Drells). Recording engineers were not satisfied, however. They wanted to hear each instrument more distinctly, so they put a mike next to each one. This technique, called "close miking," accomplished their purpose, but in the process the sound of the instrument in the air (or ambience) was lost. To counteract this, these persistent engineers came up with a way of artificially restoring this ambience.

After analyzing room ambience, they realized that the loss was due in part to the time delay between a sound leaving its source (be it voice or instrument) and its return from obstacles in its path. That is, the ear hears the sound first from its source and then again after various delays (depending on the size and shape of the acoustic space) bounced off walls, ceilings, people and objects in its path.

The number, delay time, and tonal quality of these delayed repetitions of the original sound are what allow our ears to tell our brain the size and nature of the room in which the sound is produced. Highly directional microphones placed right in front of instruments and speakers eliminated leakage from other instruments, allowing each to be isolated on its own track. Unfortunately, it also eliminated all of the room sound as well, producing a very unnatural sounding tape (when was the last time you listened to an instrument stuck directly in your ear?).

To counteract this effect, engineers came up with some effects of their own to restore the natural room ambience to close-miked instruments and vocals. Many of these effects are still in use today, and allow the guitarist to sound like he or she is playing in Madison Square Garden even in a crowded, sweaty, basement-size club.

TAPE DELAY

One of the first effects engineers discovered was *tape delay*. By running a signal into a reel-to-reel tape recorder, they were able to record it on the machine's "record" head and play it back as it passed over the same machine's "playback" head. The signal coming off the playback head was slightly delayed by the distance between the two magnetic heads. This delayed signal could be added to the original signal on the main recording to create a delay effect. By recycling the delayed signal over the record and playback heads, additional repeats could be achieved.

In this system, the length of the delay can be varied in a number of ways. The speed of the tape can be varied from 7 to 15 to 30 inches per second (ips), causing the delay time to get shorter as the speed increases. The playback head can be moved farther away from the record head to lengthen the delay. Or, multiple playback heads can be used, which also allows multiple repeats without recycling.

Engineers used this technique to create the "slap" echo used on early rockabilly recordings. This slap was a short, single delay that was mixed almost as loud as the original signal and was used more as an effect than as a means of recreating ambience. In fact, it is one of the first examples of using "effects" in recording. By recycling the repeats and mixing them a little farther back, engineers also used tape echo as a means of recreating some of the room sound lost in close miking.

Of course, as soon as guitarists started using this effect in the studio, there was a tremendous demand for a unit that could recreate the effect live. Thus, the "Echoplex" was born, beginning the long standing tradition of studio effects being produced for the mass market.

The original Echoplex was a tube-driven tape recorder with a playback head that slid along a track, making the delay time extremely variable. These units used a continual tape loop (an improvement over the studio where the tape just ran out and had to be continually rewound) and allowed infinite or "runaway" feedback (or recycling). The term "runaway" comes from the fact that the amplifier section of the tape machine reamplifies each recycled signal until you get a wall of noise that increases in volume until it jeopardizes your speakers, to say nothing of your ears. Under proper control, this runaway feedback can be used as an effect.

The late Tommy Bolin (*Deep Purple*) used to have a foot pedal to control the feedback on his Echoplex so that he could achieve the wall of noise effect and then back it off before doing any damage. Adrian Belew (*King Crimson, David Bowie, The Bears*) uses an analog delay device (see next section) on a stand and manually manipulates the feedback control to create a number of insect-type sounds.

Early tube Echoplexes create an extremely warm type of echo that still has its uses in these days of "digital this and that." These units are rare and can be expensive. In addition, the tape loops are hard to come by when they need to be replaced, and the heads must be demagnetized regularly to maintain sound quality. But, if you are trying to recreate the early fifties sound or are just looking for a warm, rich-sounding echo unit with up to 2 seconds of delay, they are still hard to beat. (Transistorized Echoplexes are cheaper and more common, but do not have the same warm sound as the tube models. They are still usable, however.)

ANALOG DELAY

The aforementioned problems with tape and tape heads led researchers to seek a way of creating the same effect using the budding transistor technology. Once they put their minds to it, they were soon able to come up with "analog" delays that eliminated the need for tapes and tape heads by passing the signal along a series of IC chips. Analog delays allowed guitarists and others to reproduce tape effects with much smaller units (tape delays were about the size of a toaster oven, early analog units more like 1 lb. candy boxes) and without hassle. They fell short only in that the sound quality of the echos diminished significantly as the delay times got longer. By the time analog delays put out much more than 500 milliseconds (half a second) of delay, even the best of them had added so much noise and unwanted distortion as to be unusable. But for many purposes, 500 milliseconds is plenty, and analog delays became practically standard equipment for studios and guitarists alike.

DIGITAL DELAY

The advent of digital technology helped solve some of the problems with analog delays. The difference between analog and digital can be very confusing. The best way to think about it is that, while *analog* units deal with the actual signal itself, *digital* units break that signal down into a digital code. They then process that code and retranslate it into signal again before sending it to the output. The encoded signal is less subject to degradation, thus allowing longer delays with less distortion.

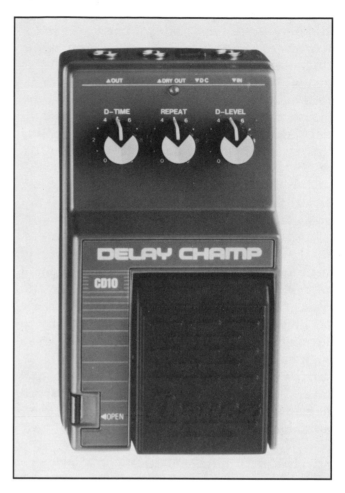

Inexpensive analog delays can sometimes provide a more natural sounding ambience than more expensive digital delays.

Digital delays allowed the possibility of delay times of 16 seconds, 32 seconds, and beyond! This in turn allows processes like sampling. While these extremely long delay times have some applications (i.e. playing along with yourself ala "Frippertronics"), the more important effect was that shorter delay times became extremely clean to the point where the delayed signal was indistinguishable from the original—a mixed blessing, as we shall see in the next section.

APPLICATIONS

As we have seen, delays can be used for ambience or effect. We will see as we progress that digital delays have not necessarily replaced analogs (just as analog did not entirely replace tape), but that each has its advantages and disadvantages.

Using delay effects can be very confusing because manufacturers seem unable to agree on terminology. Most delay units (or delay sections of multi-effects units) will have three controls. One will control the length of delay, from short to long. This may be called "Delay Time," "Effect," "Range," or simply "Delay." One will control the number of repeats, from one to "runaway." This one may be called "Feedback," "Regen." (Regeneration), or "Repeat." And one will control the amount of effect that is added to the original, or "dry" signal (a signal with no effects is called "dry"; one adds effects to make it "wetter"). This may be called "Mix," "Blend," "Delay," or "Effect," depending on the unit—thus the confusion. A short time spent playing with the unit will unravel the mystery of which control does what.

All units will have an input and an output. The signal from the guitar goes into the input, and the output is plugged into the amp or the input of the next effect. Some units will have input and output "attenuators," or volume controls. These will help you make sure that you don't send so much signal into the delay that it distorts, or so much out that you distort the next effect.

Many delays will also have a "dry" output and an "effect" output. This will allow you to send an unaffected signal to one amp or recording track, and either just the delay signal, or a blend of dry and effect signal, to another amp or track.

Creating artificial ambience with a delay unit is easy. For a small room, "hard reverb" sound (more about reverb in the next section) a short delay with a number of repeats is best. You will find that you may want quite a bit of effect signal in the mix. This will make you sound like you are playing in a garage or basement with concrete walls (hence "hard" reverb). As you increase the length of delay, the room will increase in size, but you will have to reduce the amount of effect or the repeats will obscure your original signal. You may also want to decrease the number of repeats as you increase the length of the delay.

When trying to decide how much of the effect to blend in, keep two things in mind: On one hand, as we've said before, *less is more*—too much delay will sink your guitar way back in the mix and obscure what you are trying to put across. On the other hand, when you are setting up and checking your guitar sound, it may sound like you have enough delay in the mix, but when the rest of the band starts to play, you find that your sound is too dry. So, readjust your mix settings while the band is playing.

A good rule of thumb is to back off on the amount of effect when there is no microphone in front of your amp. You may use a little more when your guitar is going through the p.a. Also remember that if you need a lot of delay for a special effect, don't be afraid to *shut it off* when you are through. And finally, remember the story at the beginning of this chapter and be prepared to add "wetness" to your signal as the club fills up.

You may find that analog delays serve better for ambient effects than the digital variety. This is because in applications of this kind, their lack of frequency response becomes a plus. Think about it: In nature, the echoes bouncing off the walls,

Digital technology allows delay times of 7.6 seconds and longer.

On this digital delay, "delay time" refers to the length of the delay; "regen." is the same as feedback, or the number of repeats, and "mix" refers to the amount of direct versus delayed signal.

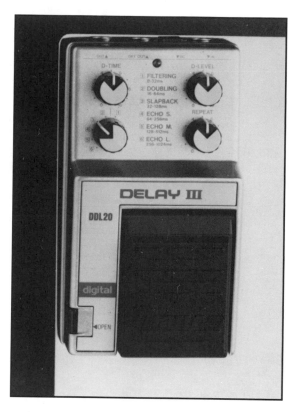

Formerly available in rack configuration only, technology has advanced to the point where digital delays and reverbs are produced in small, foot-pedal units.

etc., do not have as much high end as the original signal. With the delay lengths required for small room sounds, and even larger hall simulations, any decent analog delay will have a good enough frequency response to avoid muddying up your sound. The small amount of high end loss inherent in analog delays will be just enough to make the ambience sound natural. At shorter delay times, digital delays tend to be too clean to sound natural—the echoed sound is identical to the original signal. Some of the more expensive digital delays have high frequency roll-offs to counteract this problem, but correct me if I'm wrong to think that it's silly to pay extra to make a more expensive device sound like a much cheaper one!

Digital delays do have their place. For a doubling effect, digitals can fatten out the sound by making it sound like two guitars playing. In this case, you want the delay to be as clean as possible because you will be mixing it equally or almost with the original. For doubling, you want the delay long enough to fatten the sound, but short enough so that it is not audible as a rhythmic pattern. Also, you want to use only one repeat or it will begin to sound like "hard reverb."

Digital delays are also good for setting up rhythmic repeat patterns—a short slap with a single repeat mixed equally with the original signal can turn your guitar into a sequencer. Longer delays can create polyrhythmic patterns a la Andy Summers *(Police)*. Just remember, if you are playing with a live drummer (I've heard some people still do), he must be able to hear you because your delay time will set the tempo. (Some digital delays

allow you to change the delay length with a foot controller.)

Digital delays with longer delay times (2 seconds or more) allow you to create "Frippertronic" effects by playing along with yourself. This may be done in one of two ways: You may set the delay time at a very long time, the mix at near equal, and the feedback at just below "runaway." This way, as old patterns fade, you can overlay new ones. Or, you may use the "hold" button (present on almost all digital delays) to lock in what you have played up until that point, and then perform improvisations that will not be recorded. These improvisations may sound very dry unless you are running your guitar signal through a second delay set for a more subtle sort of ambient sound before the digital, or a reverb after it.

Speaking of reverb, this brings us to our next section.

REVERB

True ambience is never a result of a single delay length or multiple, evenly spaced repeats. Walls, floors, ceilings, and other objects are continually echoing the sound back at us at various delay times. In addition, these echoes are rarely heard individually; that is, in the average room, one does not say, ''Hello'' and hear ''Hello,'' ''Hello,'' ''Hello,'' etc. You hear the original sound in the air and identify the echoes not as repeats, but as ambience—or the size, type, and emptiness or fullness of the room in which the sound is uttered.

Delay units are limited in their ability to reproduce ambience by the distinction and the identical nature of their repeats. While they are adequate on sounds with little or no attack, like volume swells and lightly picked or strummed chords, the repeats become too distinct and the regularity of their spacing too pronounced when any hard picking or tight, funky chord work is required.

SPRING REVERBS

The first type of mechanical reverb developed was the ''spring reverb.'' This unit is found in virtually all guitar amplifiers containing reverb. The signal is converted from electrical energy to mechanical energy by one transducer, which sends it down a spring to another transducer, which converts it back to electrical energy. The time it takes to travel the length of the spring adds delay. In addition,

the spring degrades the frequency response. So far there would appear to be little difference between this and an echo unit, but the spring affects the frequency response in a more uneven manner than analog or digital delays, therefore creating a more natural effect. The more springs, the more natural the effect, and the longer the springs, the longer the delay. Spring reverbs driven by tubes offer a warmth unavailable in any but the most expensive digital reverbs. They are, however, prone to giving off a ''sproi-oi-oing'' sound when subjected to hard attack. Still, for the true Duane Eddy tone, they are unbeatable.

At their best, spring reverbs offer limited types of room simulation. The advent of digital effects gave us the digital reverb, and seemingly overnight it was possible to simulate virtually any size and type of room. In addition, digital reverbs allow you to place the sound anywhere you like in the room. You could walk in place in the studio, and an engineer miking your feet and with a digital reverb could make it sound like you are walking back and forth across the room. This technology is what gives us the airy sound of ECM jazz records (Pat Metheny, John Abercrombie, Bill Frisell, et al) and conspires with drum machines to totally eliminate the need for live drums (human feeling not withstanding).

The repeat/hold buttons on these delay units allow you to set up a delay pattern, lock it in, and then play along with it in a ''sound-on-sound'' fashion.

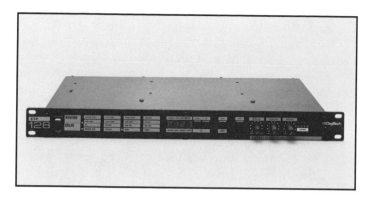

This unit allows you to get delay and reverb in a single package.

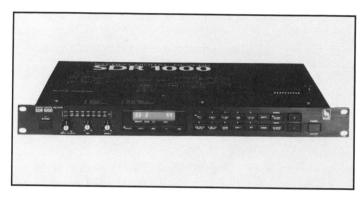

Some digital reverbs allow you to modify all the parameters of the effect. This permits creation of any size or type of room ambience.

Like digital delays, digital reverbs have become available in smaller and smaller packages. Three of these will fit in one rack space, and foot-pedal units are available as well.

MIDI reverb units allow you to select different types of reverb at the same time that you make changes on all of your other MIDI effects (see Chapter Five).

DIGITAL REVERBS

Digital reverbs, like digital delays, take the signal and convert it to digital code. They then add the various delays and frequency changes necessary to simulate the desired size room and to place the sound in the desired location within it.

The first digital reverbs were large and extremely expensive ($15,000 and up), and they remained so for about five years. Then, within the next five years the price plummeted, until (at this writing) they are available for under $140!!

APPLICATION

Reverb allows you to tailor the ambience of the room to your own design. If you are already playing in an airplane hangar or ice hockey rink, you will undoubtedly want to be very frugal in adding reverb. But, if you are in a heavily carpeted club draped with velour curtains, that is packed beyond the fire laws, feel free to lay it on with a trowel!

Many of the same rules apply as with delay—be careful not to bury yourself in the mix. However, with reverb you need not worry about affecting the rhythm by using too much, as there are no individual repeats.

CHORUS, FLANGING, AND OTHER DELAY EFFECTS

You have undoubtedly heard and enjoyed the chiming sound of a twelve string guitar, either electric or acoustic, or been impressed by the fullness of the sound created by two guitars playing the identical part at the same time. You may not have been aware, however, that the fullness and chiming characteristics that you enjoy are created by sounds that are out of synch and out of tune!

It may seem to you that the big sound is created by twice as many strings, but in reality, this has very little to do with it. The richness of the sound comes from the fact that the extra set of strings (be they, the octave strings on a twelve string or an additional six string guitar) are not played at exactly the same time or perfectly in tune with the first set.

There are a couple of ways to illustrate this. If you have access to a multi-track recorder, try recording a guitar part on one track, and then try bringing it up through another channel or bouncing it to another track. Play back both channels together. You will find that the two tracks together do not sound much bigger, if at all, than the one track alone. Now rerecord the part on a separate track. Play that one along with the original. You will hear the fullness that you are seeking because it is unlikely that you were able to play it exactly the way you played it the first time, and by now, your guitar has slipped slightly out of tune.

If a multi-track machine is unavailable, try tuning a twelve string guitar with an electronic tuner. Play it and listen. It will have the distinctive twelve string sound because of irregularities in the intonation, and the fact that your pick hits the doubled strings a millisecond apart. But, if you detune the doubled strings very slightly, you will notice that the richness of the sound actually increases as you detune the strings up until the point where it begins to sound seriously out of tune.

This phenomenon involving slight time and tuning variation is what allows chorus devices to make one gutar sound like two or make a six stringed instrument sound like a twelve stringed one.

CHORUS

A chorus device, whether an analog box or part of a rack mount digital delay, takes the signal and delays it (approximately 20 milliseconds). Where it differs from straight delay is that it constantly varies this delay time over a range of up to 5 milliseconds (plus or minus). The result will be obvious if you take any standard delay unit and play a note while turning the delay time control knob back and forth. You will hear the pitch of the note vary in an unpleasant fashion. What makes a chorus pleasing is that the variation is more minimal and is mixed in with the original signal. This simulates the effect of additional strings being played slightly out of time and tune.

Chorus effects allow one six string guitar to simulate the sound of a twelve string or two guitars playing at once.

FLANGING

The true origins of the term "flanging" have been lost in time, but the most common story is that an English engineer placed his thumb on a tape reel, or "flange" as they are known in England, observed the "whooshing" sound that was produced, and found it good. This sound was produced by his thumb causing a very short, but extremely irregular delay effect. This is simulated with flangers by sweeping a basically short delay (shorter than chorus—about 5 to 10 milliseconds) over a very wide range (from 1 to 10, or 2 to 20 milliseconds).

Flangers are often confused with phase shifters due to the similar "whooshing" sound. Phase shifters do not contain any delay electronics, but merely sweep the tone of the signal continually through the frequency spectrum—that is, from treble to bass. Flangers *do* add time delay and offer a somewhat richer and more varied sound. A phase shifter is desirable in cases where a more subtle effect is required, or where it is important that the pitch remains unaffected.

Manufacturers are a little less confusing in labeling the controls on chorus and flanging devices, but the names do vary from unit to unit. "Depth" or "width" refers to how far the delay time strays up and down from the center point. As we saw with detuning the twelve string—more equals richer until the detuning becomes unpleasant. The "speed" or "rate" knob controls how fast the time sweeps from minimum to maximum—from a long, slow sweep to a rapid Leslie speaker-type of effect. You will find that if you increase the speed, you will be able to use more depth without sounding out of tune.

Flangers have an added control marked "feedback" or "regeneration." This works the same way as on delay devices, but in this case, it increases the "metallic" sound of the effect.

Most rack mounted digital delay units (and some floor units) offer chorus and flanging capablities. The speed/rate and width/depth controls are usually grouped in a section called "modulation." Using a unit like this illustrates the fine line between chorus and flanging, since you have to set the appropriate delay times for each. You will find that different time settings will cause the modulation section to react differently, allowing you an enormous range of possible sounds. Many such units also offer "phase reversal" which affects flanging more particularly, creating extremely odd metallic effects.

Once again, analog chorus and flanging offer warmer, more natural sounding effects, while digital offers cleaner, more accurate reproduction.

There are two important advantages in using delays for chorus and flanging. In addition to the already mentioned wider range of effects, rack delays offer both input and output attenuation, whereas most floor units do not. Also—*and extremely important*, since they are a delay unit as well—these units allow you to blend the affected signal *in any desired amount with the original signal*. With most floor units you either have chorus/flanging mixed equally with the original signal, or none at all. Being able to blend it in allows you to use large amounts for maximum chime on Byrds-like fingerpicked chords, or a little less to give more ring to your strumming, or just a hint to fatten your solo sound without muddying it up or sinking it too far into the mix.

As with all the other effects we have discussed so far, *the right amount of chorus and/or flanging is essential*. Most floor units, while allowing depth and rate adjustments, do not allow you to choose the amount of effect you want blended into the mix—they are either on or off.

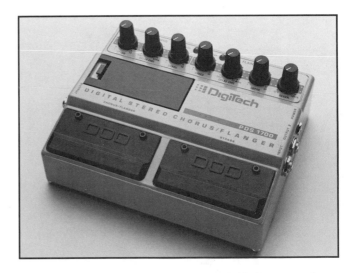

Flanging and chorusing are often available in one package.

APPLICATIONS

Chorused guitar is present on almost every modern pop record that you hear (that contains guitar). Extreme flanging is used less often, but occasionally what sounds like chorus is a mild flange with little or no regeneration. Andy Summers' chiming on early *Police* records was an Electro-Harmonix flanger set for minimal regeneration.

If a twelve string guitar sound is what you are after, use a twelve string guitar, and two guitars playing the same thing is still fuller and richer than any chorus device, but this is not always practical. In addition, the sound of chorusing has become a popular effect in its own right. The wash of chorused guitar on many modern pop records has become a standard sound in the modern guitarist's vocabulary. If you run your guitar through a chorus device, be it floor pedal or expensive rack mount, and the sound is not as full as what you hear on record, despair not. What you are hearing is often a guitar run through two or more choruses, flanging, and delay units, or overdubbed many times.

For live purposes, more often than not, one chorus will suffice—especially if used in conjunction with other effects such as compressors and delays (more on this in the next chapter).

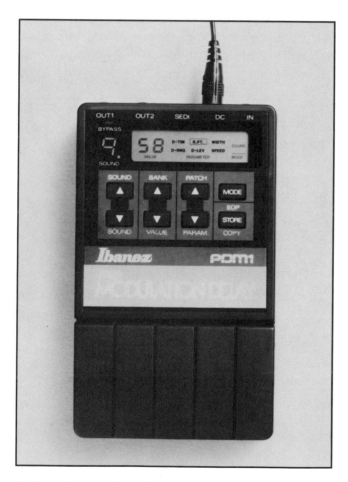

Delay units used for chorusing or flanging allow you to blend affected and unaffected signals as you wish.

Tricks
Of The
Trade

CHAPTER FIVE

Putting It All Together

IF YOU HAVE READ THIS FAR, you should have a basic understanding of how to make your guitar sound the way that you want, and how to use the five most common effects—**compression, distortion, chorus/flanging, delay, and reverb.**

The only way to increase your understanding is "hands-on" experience. Find a small, friendly music store and ask to try the effects. Go early, when they are not crowded. Play quietly and concentrate on learning about the effect—not showing off your latest licks.

Over the years I have observed Andy Summers, Peter Frampton, Brian Setzer, Mark Knopfler, Ulrich Roth, John Abercrombie, Bill Frisell, Bill Connors, Eddie Martinez, Steve Kahn, Jeff Miranov, and many other excellent professional guitarists test out equipment and guitars. Many times, to listen, you would never know that these musicians were at the top of their field. They would play one note or one basic lick over and over again, listening to the sound of the instrument, pickup, amp, or effect that they were testing.

Take your cue from them; listen for the *sound,* not the lick. If you find the sound you are looking for, buy the equipment *there* (assuming they are not outrageously overpriced). Don't go to another store just to save a dollar or two. Stores that concentrate on lower prices may not be as interested in service. If you take a salesman's time trying out his product and then buy it elsewhere, he may not be as ready to take the time with you in the future. And, the store that offers the best price may not be as receptive if you have any problems with the product.

An ideal situation is to find a friend with the piece of gear that interests you. You might even be able to borrow it to use on a gig (some stores offer this service—take advantage of it!).

You may be wondering about some effects that I have not mentioned or that have been only briefly discussed. Some, such as volume and wah-wah pedals, I feel are simple and self-explanatory, or very limited in application, such as envelope followers, frequency analyzers, or harmonizers. Information is available on these effects elsewhere (see bibliography). More importantly, you will find that 90 out of 100 guitar sounds that you hear live and on record can be reproduced using some combination of the "Big Five" (*compression, distortion, chorus/flanging, delay,* and *reverb).*

While we are discussing omissions, you may feel that I have left out an important guitarist's tool —the *guitar synthesizer.* In fairness, I must confess to having mixed emotions regarding these units. Part of me says, "If you want a synthesizer, play a keyboard," and part of me says that the guitar synth opens a new world of sound to the guitarist.

The main reason I have omitted the guitar synthesizer here is that the world of sounds that it opens are not *guitar sounds* per se. My concern in this book is for the reader to get the most expression out of the guitar while still retaining the distinctive characteristics that we look for when we decide to play guitar, and not keyboards.

Aside from the fact that guitar synthesizers could take up another book (and probably will), in my opinion, guitar synthesizers are woefully lacking in allowing the characteristics of the guitar to come through (attack, string bending, etc). This will undoubtedly improve, but there will always be a place for the unsurpassed expressiveness of the minimally adorned electric guitar. This is one reason I stress moderation in the use of effects, and will continue to do so as we proceed.

The "Chain of Command"

One of the most frequently asked questions that I have encountered is, "Which effect goes before which?" There are rules that can help you decide.

Compressors, as a rule, should come first in the chain. This means that you should run the cable from your guitar into the input of the compressor. As we discussed, while compressors do not necessarily add noise themselves, they will raise the noise level of everything before them. In addition, we saw that it is desirable to send an even signal to your other effects.

Next should come your *distortion* effect, since you want to distort the purest signal that you can before sending it on for further processing. You can hear the difference for yourself. Try putting a chorus or delay before the distortion and then after it. The latter will result in a less muddy sound. It will also result in less noise. Since distortion units add so much gain, like compressors, they will increase the noise of anything before them in the chain.

These rules apply to using amp distortion as well. If you are in love with the sound of your amp distortion, there are a couple of ways to arrange it before the rest of your effects.

If your amp features an effects loop, the odds are that its distortion stage is before the loop (check to be sure). As I mentioned earlier, you must be very careful with effects loops. If the "line out" level can be matched with the input of your effects, you are in business. You simply run the line level out into your next effect, and run out of the output of your last effect back into the input of the loop. This is where the input and output attenuators on rack mounted units come into play. Some amps step the output level of their loops down to instrument level, allowing you to use floor effects.

Keep in mind that if you use floor effects, you must run a cable from the line out to the front of the stage where you can step on your effects, and then back to the input. This is a lot of cable and can affect your tone.

If this seems like more trouble than it is worth, or your effects loop does not match level with your effects, do not despair. It is still possible to use your amp distortion in front of your effects. More and more studio pros and touring musicians are running out of the effects loop's line out (or any line output either provided with the amp or installed by an amp repairman) and into a multi-channel mixer. They then run each of their effects into its own channel—or two channels for stereo

Many amplifiers offer effects loops that allow you to place the amplifier distortion before the rest of your effects.

(more on this later). This allows the distortion to come either from the preamp or main amp stage.

If the main amp is used, the power must be attenuated to line level to avoid blowing up the mixer and the effects, and a "dummy" resistance load must replace the speakers. For the same reason— **DON'T EVER PLUG INTO AN EFFECT FROM THE SPEAKER OUTPUT.** In fact, **DON'T EVER PLUG INTO ANYTHING FROM THE SPEAKER OUTPUT EXCEPT THE PROPER RESISTANCE SPEAKERS OR A POWER ATTENUATOR.** This includes mixers, effects, headphones, tape recorders, etc.

When using a mixer with your amplifier, you must then use one or more additional clean power amps to bring your volume back up to stage level. This method is expensive because you are, in effect, using an entire amplifier as a distortion box. It will, however, result in a terrific sound. It allows you to simulate studio conditions where your amp distortion is unaffected until it goes through the board.

Assuming for the moment that you are using effects linked together in series (one into the next), the next device after distortion is normally *chorus/flanging.* Since it uses such a short delay time, it does not degrade the signal as much as longer delay effects, and thus sends the cleanest signal to the next effect. An exception to this positioning rule would be if you are using the chorus to split the signal for stereo. In that case, you would use it last in the chain before the amps.

Next would come any short *delays* for doubling or slap effects, and then any longer ambient or "spacey" types of delays.

Finally comes *reverb,* usually by necessity because it is in the amplifier, but also for naturalness of sound.

As with most rules, these rules have exceptions. In some cases, you may want to have your delay before your distortion. If you set the delay for a mild effect for rhythm work, you will notice that when you switch on your distortion for lead, the delay effect becomes much more pronounced. When using a minimal amount of distortion, and a quality delay, this can sound quite good (not too muddy). What you achieve is not having to step on two buttons in order to have delay on your lead. The delay is already on, but is far less noticeable in the rhythm mode.

The only hard and fast rule is, "If it sounds good—do it!" Feel free to experiment with different effects in different places in the chain. The above is just a guideline to what has been proven effective, but for special sounds—anything goes.

Stereo

WARNING — ONCE YOU HAVE HEARD YOUR GUITAR IN STEREO, IT IS HARD TO GO BACK TO MONO. I issue this warning because once you make the commitment to stereo, you are talking about transporting a minimum of two amplifiers, often three! This involves much lifting (unless you can afford roadies). In the studio, it involves two tracks for each of your guitar parts, which can result in much arguing with engineers and other band members (unless you are a star). In spite of these drawbacks, I am sure you will agree that once you have heard yourself in stereo, it is hard to go back to mono.

Playing in stereo involves splitting one guitar signal into two. There are a number of ways to do this—you will decide for yourself which you prefer.

Just using a Y-cord is not enough. For the reasons we discussed in the section on chorus, running the same signal into two amps or tracks does not sound significantly bigger than one. It is therefore necessary to process at least one of the signals to differentiate it from the other.

You can hear this difference by using the first method of stereo splitting—*delay.* You need a delay unit that has a "direct" out and an "effect" out. The "effect" out should allow you to remove all of the direct signal with the blend control, leaving only the delayed signal. Put this unit last in the chain, even after the reverb (if it is external). Run one cable out of the "direct" out into one amp or track, and another cable out of the "effect" out into the other amp or track. Set the blend (or effect, or delay, depending on the make of the unit) so that only delayed signal is coming out of the "effect" output. Set the delay length at 0, then gradually increase it. Stop and play at regular intervals. It takes only a very short delay time to make your guitar sound huge. As you increase the delay time, you will notice the sound get bigger and bigger until the delay starts to sound like a slap. You want to avoid a delay length that is so long it affects the rhythm (except for special effects).

Try adding a chorus effect and a longer ambient delay before splitting the signal. Kick in the compressor, strike a ringing chord, then rock your tremelo arm a little. This is a sound you hear on many modern records—now you know why! It sounds immense!

Now shut off the splitting delay and play again. Even though you are playing through two amps or tracks, the sound shrinks tremendously. You now know why it is hard to go back to mono.

A second stereo method uses *chorus*. Many chorus units offer mono and stereo outputs; however, the function of these outputs varies with different manufacturers. In some, one output is direct signal and the other is direct and effect mixed. In others, both outputs are a blend of direct and affected signal, but the pitch shifting on one side is out of phase with the pitch shifting on the other side. This provides a very rich stereo chorus effect when used with two amplifiers. If you attempt to get this effect by running each output into a different input of the same amp, you may run into problems. One side will be telling the speaker to go one way, while the other output tells it to go the other way.

If you use only a chorus to split your signal, you are committed to having this effect *on* at all times or losing the stereo effect. There are, however, a number of other ways to achieve stereo using chorus.

One involves using a digital delay that offers pitch modulation. You run a cable from the "direct" out to one amp, and a cable from the "effect" or "mix" out to the other. As with using delay to split the signal, make sure only the affected signal

is coming out of the effect side. Now add a little pitch modulation to that side and you will have a stereo sound with a mild doubling effect that you can leave on at all times. Should you occasionally find even this much pitch shift to be more than you want, you can remove it and still have a stereo effect using only delay. (Many programmable and MIDI digital delays will allow you to make this change by just switching programs with your foot.)

Unless your digital processor offers phase reversed stereo chorusing, this last method will only give you effect on one side, and direct on the other. If your equipment is less "state of the art," don't despair. You can still have "true" stereo chorusing (phase reversed) *and* the option of shutting it off without losing your stereo sound. It is just a question of routing.

All you need is a "true" stereo chorus and any delay that offers a "direct" out and an "effect" out. It is not necessary to use an expensive delay unit, as we are dealing in such a short delay that almost any unit will sound good. Just be sure that by manipulating the blend control, you are able to get *just* delay out of the "effect" out.

This illustrates one possible method of playing in stereo. If you can get your stereo chorusing from a programmable delay, you can switch from chorus to a short delay without losing your stereo effect.

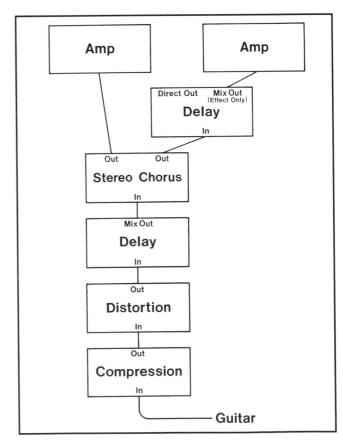

This routing allows you to shut off your chorus and maintain your stereo imaging (without a programmable delay).

Run your signal into the input of the stereo chorus. Now run a cable out of one of the chorus outputs into one of the amps. Then run another cable out of the other chorus output into the input of the delay. Finally, run a cable out of the "effect" out of the delay into the other amp.

Set the delay for as much as you need for a stereo effect without the chorus, and leave it on. You now have the option of adding "true" stereo chorus or not without losing the bigness of stereo.

Yet another means of creating a stereo effect is to use *digital reverb*. Many of these units offer stereo inputs as well as outputs. This allows you to run different signals into each input and keep them separate. For example, you may want to run your direct signal to one side, and an unaffected signal blended with a long delay in the background to the other. Or, you may run the two outputs of a stereo chorus into the two inputs of the stereo digital reverb.

For those of you with a large budget, there is the *mixer method* that we discussed in the section on distortion. By using three amplifiers and a stereo mixer with eight or more channels, you can have a stage setup that rivals any studio sound. You can route your amplifier and effects through the mixer's effects loops and different channels, and then send the stereo signal to two power amps. This will allow you to pan your effects right, left, or anywhere in between. It also allows you to blend in any amount of any effect you like.

If you are on a somewhat limited budget, or lack space in the van for two or three amplifiers, don't be discouraged. Unless you are playing large concert venues with stereo p.a.'s or small clubs with no microphones on the amps, a stereo stage setup is really for your ears only. As far as the audience is concerned, that stereo spread turns into mono a few rows from the stage, and a mono p.a. will turn that expensive stereo sound right back into mono.

This is not to say that you should take *your* ears lightly. Our whole credo herein is that if you sound good to *you*, it will help you play better. So if you can afford it, and you are willing to haul it (or pay to have it hauled), by all means, *go stereo!*

Switching

Remember way back in the guitar section we discussed the compromise that often needs to be made between having the maximum number of sounds available, and the requirements of stage performance. Until the early eighties, these same considerations applied to the use of effects.

Once your stage setup involves two or more effects, you have to start doing a little dance. For example, if you want to shut off your chorus and turn on your distortion before your solo, you must leave yourself time to step on two pedals. As the number of pedals increases, so does the choreography. Perhaps you want to turn on your distortion and a long delay while turning off your compressor and chorus. You could start to look like you are stamping out a fire!

An early solution was the Boss computerized switching system, and early systems by people like Pete Cornish in England and Bob Bradshaw in America. These systems allowed players like Adrian Belew, Andy Summers, and Steve Lukather to turn on a number of effects at the same time by just stepping on one button. They offered pre-set combinations so that by stepping on one pedal, players could turn on two or more effects while shutting others off.

The advent of programmable effects brought on a new problem. New digital effects—delays, reverbs, multi-effects (like the Yamaha SPX-90)—allowed you to get different sounds from the same unit at the switch of a program. You could, for example, program three different length delays, a chorus sound, and a flanging sound into a digital unit and then recall each of them by pushing one button or stepping on a pedal.

This was wonderfully convenient in that you no longer had to manually change all the parameters (and remember them) each time you wanted a new sound. Unfortunately, it added an additional step to the effects switching dance. You now had to not only turn the unit on and off, but also select the appropriate program.

MIDI

With the ever faster technological advances, the solution to the problems of effects switching came within a few years. The answer was **MIDI**.

To keep it very simple, MIDI (Musical Instrument Digital Interface) is an electronic language that allows different electronic devices to talk to one another—even if they are made by different manufacturers. In practical terms, this means that effects-switching units can not only turn effects on and off, but also choose different programs at the same time. You can now turn on your distortion, turn off your compressor, change your delay from short to long, change your reverb from "large hall" to "small room," and do it all by stepping on *one* button.

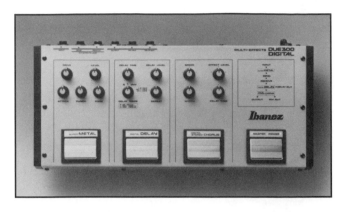

Multi-effects units offer compactness and rapid setup time.

Programmable effects allow parameters to be stored and recalled for a variety of sounds. MIDI allows you to switch any number of devices on and change their parameters at the same instant.

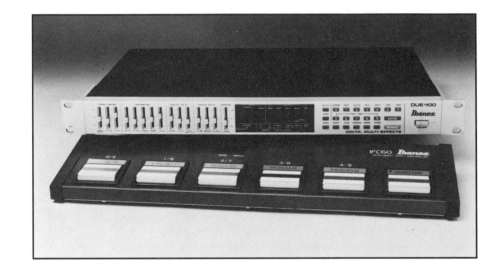

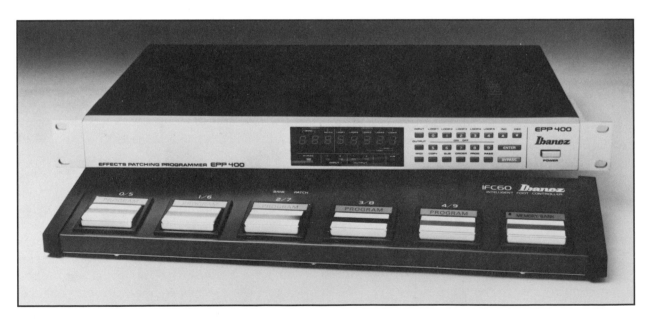

An effects patching programmer makes it possible to switch combinations of effects in and out of your signal path by simply stepping on one pedal.

As of this writing, switching systems that allow you to mix MIDI and non-MIDI effects cost thousands of dollars. I am absolutely sure that very soon this will change. For one thing, it is just a matter of time before all rack mountable effects are MIDI and you will no longer need to have complex systems that mix MIDI and non-MIDI.

Even as I write, Roland offers a multi-effects rack that offers programmable distortion, chorus/flanging, delay, reverb, and others all in one unit for a reasonable price. The only drawback of multi-effects units is that while you may like the sound of the chorus on one unit, you might prefer another manufacturer's distortion.

As more and more effects become available in MIDI format, you will be able to use your favorite manufacturer for each effect, and they will all be switchable and programmable by stepping on one button. In fact, if you are playing music that uses MIDI drum machines, sequencers, and synthesizers, it is entirely possible to program your effects changes into the sequencer, hook your switcher into the system, and have your effects change at the appropriate place in each song *without ever having to step on any buttons!!*

When Not To Use Effects

You may have heard the expression, "If you are not part of the solution, you are part of the problem." While this makes for an overly simplistic political philosophy, it can stand you in good stead as a guideline for using effects. Add only those that add to the music—if they don't add, they subtract.

First consider the musical context. Does this type of music call for this effect? If the sound is Chicago blues, is a stereo chorus really necessary? If the sound is "in your face" speed metal, won't a lot of chorus and long echoes soften the sound too much? Wouldn't distortion and a hard reverb be enough? Obviously, these are judgment calls, and as such, are highly subjective. But the bottom line is: Use an effect if you think the music needs it—not just because it is there!

Next, consider what I will call the "ambience context." If you are playing a large echo-filled auditorium to a half empty (O.K., let's be optimistic—half *full*) house, the last thing you need to add is large amounts of reverb. Even within the band, if you are playing with a keyboard player who favors string sounds and a drummer who just loves his ride cymbal, a drier sound will help you cut through.

Andy Summers was able to develop a sound built on flangers and delays, in a large part, because he was in a three-piece band with a drummer who laid heavily on snare, toms, and high hat. This left a big sonic space for Andy's effects.

Once again, many of the sound subtlties that you hear on stage are lost out in the audience. This is where taping your rehearsals and shows comes in handy. From where you are standing, those chorused, flanged, echoed, reverbed washes of open chords may sound beautiful, but the tape may reveal that they are just noise when mixed with the keyboards and drums.

Guitar solos, in particular, fall prey to the "more is less" syndrome. While practicing leads in your room, all that distortion, chorusing, echoing, and doubling gives a full sound that makes up for the band that isn't there. When the band *is* there, however, all those effects sink you so far into the mix that your brilliant musical ideas are reduced to background noise.

Great guitar sound cannot be bought by adding more and more expensive effects to an expensive guitar. It comes from taking the instrument and effects at hand and using them in the *most musical way possible* within the context of the band and the room.

Finally, consider your musical identity. Now that you have hundreds of sounds at your disposal, as well as the ability to call them up with one stomp on a pedal, there is an overwhelming temptation to use them. Obviously, you wish to use whichever effects will make the song sound better. But within those parameters, there is a large range of possibilities. Changing sounds four or five times in a song, and dozens of times over the course of a set, is fine if you are trying to reproduce top forty tunes or satisfy a producer as a studio musician. If, however, you have your own band and are interested in developing your own sound, it can be difficult to do when that sound changes every eight bars.

It may seem that artists like Adrian Belew and Andy Summers have been able to use a wide range of effects while still maintaining a strong identity. Close examination of their styles will reveal, however, that they continually return to a few sounds that have become identified with them.

I am sure that you, too, will find yourself returning to a few sounds that you like, and this will help you develop your own sound. Furthermore, these sounds will inspire your musical ideas. Just remember—*sounds are not a substitute for ideas!*

CHAPTER 6
Live vs. The Studio

GETTING A GREAT GUITAR SOUND in the recording studio can be a guitarist's biggest nightmare! You have worked years to achieve what you consider to be a great live sound, and your opinion has been confirmed by objective listeners. You enter a recording studio, lay down your tracks, then go into the control booth and listen to the results—*aaaaarrrgh!* What is that thin, awful sound? Who is that playing?

This scene is played out in studios around the world every day. Somewhere between your amplifier speakers and the playback speakers, your sound is destroyed. This has happened to me many times over the years. For the first few years I thought it was me—then I learned. Here are some tips.

Ideally, when you record your guitar, you should be able to perform with your sound and have that sound transferred to tape. Unfortunately, unless you are doing a big budget album, the circumstances are usually less than ideal.

For starters, when you are recording your rhythm tracks, the trick is to isolate your guitar from the other instruments as completely as possible. Some studios will have separate rooms for your amplifier where you can turn up as loud as you like without leaking into the drum microphones. Most will not.

Another isolation method is *baffling*, which involves building a little room around your amp and usually requires greatly reduced volume. A third method is going directly from your guitar (and effects, if any) into the board.

The second and third methods can seriously compromise your sound. A good portion of the sound character of an electric guitar comes from the sound produced by the speaker in the air. Baffling requires putting the microphone quite close to the amp, a place where you rarely put your ears, and can therefore produce an unpleasant sound. Going direct eliminates the sound in the air completely, as well as eliminating the speaker itself.

If you are lucky, these guitar tracks will be disposable and used just to help get the bass and drums down, and hopefully, you will have the opportunity to redo them. If time and budget won't permit this, you must try to get as good a sound as you can under the circumstances.

Try to hear a playback of your sound before you go for a good take. If it doesn't sound right, try to explain to the engineer what is missing—highs, lows, midrange, etc. Be diplomatic but persistent. Do not accept the explanation that they will "fix it in the mix."

Unless you are going to have a say in the mixing process, it is a good idea to get as many of the effects as you need right on the track, or at least printed on a separate track. Producers sometimes like to record a dry sound and add the effects later, so that all of the effects on each of the instruments blend properly, and in an ideal situation this is the best method. But often, mix time comes and there are not enough effects to go around, and the digital delay that you wanted for your solo's echo is being used for a slap for the vocals.

So, if you are sure you want a certain effect on your guitar, try and put it down when you record. If there are enough tracks to put the effect on its own track, the producer will have the option of blending in as much or as little as is required in the mix, but will not have to tie up a device to do it. If there are not enough tracks to print the effects separately, you must try to record them on your track or trust the producer's discretion.

When it is time to do overdubs, whether to replace the basic guitar or to add parts or solos, there are a few other things to consider.

Many otherwise state-of-the-art studios have less than hi-fi quality cue systems. Their headphones are big, unwieldy, and distort easily. When you finally have the whole room to yourself and can crank up your amp to get the sound that you want, you find that they cannot make the rhythm tracks loud enough in your headset. The headphone cable keeps getting entangled in your guitar cable, and on top of that, every time you want to hear a playback, you have to take off the headphones, take off your guitar, and go into the booth. It is difficult to be brilliantly creative under these conditions!

The solution is to do your overdubs in the control booth with the engineer. This allows you to hear your guitar coming out of the speakers along with the tracks, exactly as it will sound on tape. Aside from all of the other difficulties with headphones, they do not give you a good representation of what your guitar sounds like.

If you work in the booth, it is best to have your amp head and all of your effects in the booth so that you can tweak your sound right there. If the engineer can stand to raise the monitoring volume high enough, it is even possible to do feedback effects.

Back when we were baffling in basic tracking, I mentioned that placing the microphone too close can create an undesirable sound. One mistake many engineers make is to place the mike facing directly into the center of the speaker cone, which can result in a very thin, trebly sound that no amount of mixing board equalization can mend.

A little common sense will tell you that the sound that you hear from an amplifier is the dispersion of the whole speaker, coupled with the reverberation of the room. When overdubbing, it is desirable to place as many mikes as possible around the room, as well as close to the speakers, but off-center.

By mixing these sounds together you can achieve a great natural sound, as well as some great, unnatural sounds if this is what you prefer. If you find a particular microphone and/or placement that you like, write it down so that you do not forget and can request it at your next session.

THE "ROCKMAN" REVOLUTION

Undoubtedly, guitarist Tom Scholz, the brains behind the group *Boston*, went through many of the experiences previously described. His solution was to invent a box the size of a personal stereo that would allow him and other guitarists to obtain a great sound by simply plugging into the mixing board of a recording studio. He attempted to eliminate the need for amplifiers, microphones, and a whole slew of effects.

His little box, the "Rockman," combined the "Big Five" (compression, distortion, chorus, and delay/reverb) in one package. He also adjusted the equalization so that the normally thin direct sound would have some body. Used with headphones, his little device allowed silent practicing as well.

In this era of drum machines, synth-basses, and synthesizers, the Rockman removed almost entirely the need for microphones or performance rooms in recording studios. Now almost everything could go directly into the mixing board (there are still vocals on some records).

In all fairness, the Rockman revolution allows the guitarist to go into the recording studio and instantly attain an acceptable sound, much in the same way that electronic drums (Simmons and the like) eliminate the hours of miking and beating on acoustic drums normally required to achieve a respectable sound.

The downside is that, as with electronic drums, the sound lacks any individuality. The compression in the Rockman cannot be shut off, with the attendant problems previously discussed in the section on compression. There are two clean and two distorted sounds, but the parameters are all fixed. On the more expensive Rockman, you may shut off the chorus or the delay/reverb, but not both, and the parameters are fixed there as well. In other words, everyone who uses a Rockman will sound very similar.

For recording purposes, the cheaper Rockman "Soloist" is in some ways preferable. It allows you to shut off both the delay (a stereo slap) and chorus, and run a dry (albeit compressed) signal. To this you may add your own desired reverb and delay, and thus individualize your sound.

A friend once said that in the studio, "The quality of your sound is limited by your engineer's ears—if he or she can't hear it, you can't get it." This is very true. Unless you are in a position to engineer your own sound, you must try to communicate to the engineer what you want. To this end, the more you can learn about the recording process, the better. It is more effective to be able to say "I want more 4k" than "Give me some more mids," or "I would like a 10 millisecond delay split in stereo," rather than "Make it sound big."

You should always try to remain diplomatic in the studio. The engineer should be your friend—not your enemy. But be assertive. Remember, most of the people who hear the finished tape will say that either the guitar sounds great or the guitar sounds lousy—not that the engineering was great or lousy. The ultimate responsibility for your sound rests with *you*.

The home recording engineer's friend—the Scholz Rockman.

A Final Note

SOME YEARS AGO, I saw Robben Ford, the noted blues/jazz guitarist, perform at the now defunct Seventh Avenue South club in New York City. Robben was known at that time for his L.A. sound; that sweet, singing tone heard on records made in Los Angeles. You know the sound—Larry Carlton had it, Jay Graydon had it, Lee Ritenour had it. Some said Robben helped originate it. It was a sound that seemed inseparably tied to a semi-hollow Gibson 335 played straight through a Mesa Boogie tube amplifier.

Well, on this particular night, Robben did occasionally play a 335. More often, though, he played a solid body Yamaha through a transistor Yamaha amp. Was his sound any different? Not much. Why? Because, much as I hate to say it, after you have waded through all of this information on pickups, strings, effects, and amps, *his sound is mostly in his fingers, and so is yours!*

How hard or softly your fingers attack the fretboard, and how hard or softly your pick, fingers, or nails pluck the strings affects your sound more than all the of digital devices in your local music store. Your vibrato and angle of pick attack will do more to develop your own sound than all the amps available.

It is easy to neglect this part of your sound and to believe that great tone can be bought. Sorry, it can't. You can buy an old Strat, a Super Reverb, and a tube distortion. You can string it up with .013's and raise the action. But you won't sound like Stevie Ray Vaughn until you put in as much practice and listening time as he has—*and maybe not even then.*

Of course, the idea is *not* to sound like Stevie Ray Vaughn or any one else. The idea is to sound like the best *you* that you can. This, too, cannot be bought; if it could, someone else could buy it and sound just like you.

By practicing acoustically, you will develop a sound in your fingers that will express your music without electricity. Once you have your sound in your head, in your heart, and in your fingers, all the rest—pickups, amplifiers, effects—should only be used to enhance that sound, not to detract from it.

How Did They Get That Sound?

ERIC CLAPTON

The sound of rock guitar took a quantum leap forward when Eric plugged his Les Paul Gibson straight into a Marshall 50 watt combo amp and turned up the volume. Over the years he has used a variety of guitars and amps, but his sound remains recognizable due to his distinctive attack and finger vibrato. His use of the two pickup Stratocaster sound actually predates Mark Knopfler's, but since he used a more distorted version, it is not a sound we associate with him.

JIMI HENDRIX

Most people think of Jimi Hendrix as an early heavy metal guitarist. The truth of the matter is, many of his tunes were built around clean or only slightly distorted rhythm parts—"All Along The Watchtower" had an *acoustic* guitar as the base. He favored the neck pickups of his various Stratocasters for both lead and rhythm work. A listen to "Little Wing" will reveal that he, too, predates Mr. Knopfler in using the "out-of-phase" sound. Both he and Clapton were using this sound long before five position switches were available. They were required to catch their three position switches in between two pickup settings.

Jimi's effects included a fuzztone (so that he could switch easily from loud, clean rhythm to distorted lead), a flanger, a wah-wah pedal, and a tape echo.

ANDY SUMMERS
(Police)

Andy helped revolutionize the sound of guitar on pop records using a few basic effects: An MXR (now re-released by Dunlop) Dynacomp compressor, into an Electro-Harmonix (no longer in business) flanger, through an analog delay and an Echoplex (no longer in business) tape delay. He amplified his sound through one or more Marshall amplifiers. The flanger was set for minimal regeneration, causing it to sound more like a chorus. For his relatively few standard guitar solos, he added an MXR Distortion Plus.

He often used two delays at once to set up polyrhythmic effects. All of these effects were controlled by a pedal board built by Pete Cornish in England.

On later albums, he began to use a guitar synthesizer. And to reproduce studio overdubs live, he would use bass pedals to control a synthesizer while he played guitar.

ADRIAN BELEW
(David Bowie, Talking Heads, solo artist, The Bears)

Mr. Belew has produced some outstanding examples of effects used to create interesting sounds. His system includes an MXR Dynacomp and graphic equalizers, ADA flanger, Big Muff fuzz tone, Polychorus, Graphic Fuzz, 16 second digital delay, Frequency Analyzer (a ring modulator), (these last five by Electro-Harmonix), and a Foxx fuzztone, as well as various other delays, both digital and analog. He also uses various guitar synthesizers, but what is interesting about him is the non-guitar-like sounds that he can get without resorting to synths.

He gets most of his amazing sounds—even the weirdest of them—using only three or four effects at a time. His compressor is on at all times, to which he will add a fuzz and flanger to get elephant or rhinocerous sounds. Or, he will rub a slide along the strings and add a touch of echo, while manipulating his volume control, to create the crying of seagulls.

EDDIE VAN HALEN

Eddie is a direct descendant of the Eric Clapton school of sound—guitar into amp! Though he may have a more sophisticated set-up these days, when he broke on the scene with his revolutionary sound, it came entirely from his fingers. His homemade guitar contained one Seymour Duncan humbucking pickup, and a non-locking tremelo!

In the studio they probably added some ambient delay, and the occasional jet plane, flanging effect, but little else. Eddie Van Halen is a perfect example of how many sounds can be wrenched from an electric guitar overdriving an amp and little else. His one pickup is not even a particularly "hot" one. This allows the articulation of his notes to come through—even at his blinding speed—without muddying up the sound.

THE EDGE
U2

U2's three piece sound is filled out rhythmically and melodically by the use of polyrhythmic echoes. The Edge follows in the tradition of Andy Summers in running his Gibson Explorer, or Fender Stratocaster, through multiple delay devices. These set up rhythms and counterrhythms fill the space left by the bass and drums.

MARK KNOPFLER
(Dire Straits)

Mark Knopfler, the man most closely associated with the so-called "out-of-phase" Stratocaster sound, has rarely played an actual Fender Stratocaster. His main guitars are old Schecter Custom Shop Strat copies, and Strat-type Pensa-Suhr guitars. As much of his distinctive sound comes from the fact that he plays with his fingers, without a pick, as from any particular guitar or pickup combination.

"Money For Nothing" was played on a Gibson Les Paul through a Jim Kelly amp (no longer available). On stage, Mark often uses a Steinberger guitar instead of the Les Paul.

RY COODER

For rhythm work, Ry plays through an old Roland chorus-vibrato pedal (no longer available) into either a Dumble, Fender, or Musicman amp. His modified Stratocasters usually have a lap steel pickup in the bridge and a humbucker in the middle. He uses a heavy glass slide through a compressor and flat wound strings.

PAT METHENEY

Pat achieves his large spacey sound by triamping. He runs his Gibson 175 through a digital delay into one Acoustic amp, out of the delay output, and into another digital delay. Out of that delay's direct out, he goes into another acoustic amp and out of the delay's effect out, into a third amp. A little pitch modulation gives him that chiming sound.

JOHN ABERCROMBIE

John, Pat Metheney, and Bill Frisell are all occasional labelmates at ECM records. ECM is known for its lush, digitally reverbed sound. John was one of the first guitarists to use a digital reverb in a live situation to reproduce that sound. He plays an Ibanez "Gibson-type" solid body guitar through a lexicon digital reverb.

BILL FRISELL

If you haven't heard of Bill Frisell, don't worry—you will. If guitar has a future, he is it. Imagine "Jim Hall meets Jimi Hendrix" or "Pat Metheney meets Jeff Beck." Bill's unique sound comes from a Gibson SG with one Seymour Duncan JB pickup run into a compressor, a volume pedal, and into an Electro-Harmonix Deluxe Memory Man analog delay/chorus/vibrato. This last unit is set for a longer delay than would usually be used for vibrato to give Bill his distinctive, slightly dissonant sound. He is also unique in that he rarely hits a note or chord head on, but rather swells into it with the volume pedal. Frisell also uses an Electro-Harmonix 16 second digital delay to set up tape-type loops (Adrian Belew does likewise).

As an astute record reviewer said of Mr. Frisell, "Oh, you could get yourself [the effects listed] and run through a 1-12 Marshall Jubilee amp—but that wouldn't necessarily make you sound like him. Frisell's genius is a matter of intuition and sensitivity, not aerobic gimmics." I couldn't have said it better myself. Check Frisell out to see how a guitarist can use an array of effects without being used by them.

The Vintage Advantage

OVER THE YEARS, the controversy has raged between musicians who claim, "The older equipment from the fifties and sixties sounds better than the new stuff," and the ones who maintain, "Modern technology can reproduce any of those sounds." As they said in the old Certs commercial, "Stop, you are both right."

Modern technology *can* undoubtedly reproduce most of the sounds that vintage lovers are seeking. The problem is that, more often than not, it *doesn't!* This is why guitarists continue to haunt vintage shops, shows, and garage sales in search of guitars, amplifiers, and effects (yes, effects!) from the fifties and sixties.

What does this equipment have that is missing in the high-tech eighties? The word you will hear most often is "warmth." Some might even claim that this is true of the music and society at large as well. But leaving sociophilosophical musings aside for a moment, this "warmth" can be broken down into technical terms. Equalization, magnetic fields, and distortion curves all play a part. And even if the magical properties of vintage equipment are not fully understood, they can be copied directly—to a point.

VINTAGE GUITARS

Why do guitarists pay $2,500 to $10,000 (current market prices) for fifties and sixties Fenders, and over $10,000 for sunburst, flame-top, '59 GibsonLes Pauls? Sound is only one reason. Rarity and even fad and fashion play a part when you are discussing vintage guitars.

For our purposes, we will concentrate on the first reason—*sound.* What do these guitars have that you can't get today. Nothing! You could have a guitar made just like them. First, you would start with lightweight, aged wood—difficult to find, and expensive when you do. Then you would finish the body and neck with nitro-cellulose lacquer to allow it to breathe—a time consuming, costly process. Next, it would be assembled by hand. Finally, you would hand over close to $2000 for it ($5000 for a '59 Paul copy).

"Fine," you say, "$2000 is still better than $2500, and $5000 is better than $10,000!" In that respect, you are correct. But consider two things before you run out and have a vintage copy custom built.

1) Remember what we learned in the section on necks. It would be a shame to spend $2000 on a custom guitar, only to have to replace a warped neck within the first year. Even if it is guaranteed, who needs the aggravation? This is not to say that all new necks will warp—most will not. But, a vintage piece offers a better guarantee than any piece of paper—if it hasn't warped in twenty or thirty years, it isn't going to!

2) If you turn around and sell a custom guitar the day after you buy it, you are selling a used guitar. As such, the price goes down one-third to one-half. After many years of playing, a vintage piece remains a vintage piece, and the odds are that the price you can ask will be more than what you paid for it.

This presupposes that you keep the guitar as original as when you bought it. If you change anything, keep the original parts so that it can be restored. For example, if you must have a hot humbucker in the bridge position of your '59 Sunburst Strat, try a Seymour Duncan Hot Rails. It can be installed without routing the body, and routing that body could knock up to $1,000 off the value of that guitar. There are many replacement parts available for vintage instruments that allow you to restore them to original before reselling.

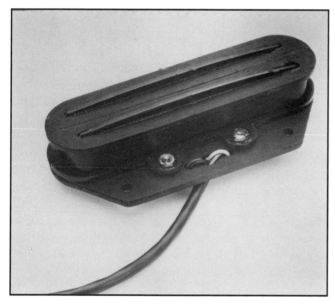

*This Hot Rails by Seymour Duncan will give you a humbucker sound without destroying the resale value of an otherwise all original 1957 Stratocaster (assuming you keep the pickup that you replace). (**Hint:** Try wiring it to a push-pull pot that will switch it from series to parallel, or a pot that will blend it from single to double coil.*

For players, as opposed to collectors, originality is not as important. This can help the guitarist interested in a reliable, playable, great sounding instrument find a bargain. A fifties or sixties Fender or Gibson that is not all original can cost thousands of dollars less than one that is.

However, you must beware of changes that can affect the sound—different pickups, Kahler or Floyd Rose bridge modifications, and, to a lesser extent, body refinishing (if it is not nitro-cellulose). On the other hand, such changes as new tuners, new vintage style bridges, neck refretting and refinishing, and decals missing will alter the sound very little, but may alter the price significantly in your favor as the buyer.

One thing that I have noticed over the years is that guitarists, as a rule, tend to be a tight-fisted bunch. Drummers think nothing of paying over $1000 for a new kit. Professional string players (violinists, cellists, etc.) may have to spend from $5000 to $25,000 for a quality instrument! And these days, poor keyboard players, if they are to remain state-of-the-art, must spend the equivalent of the annual budget of some foreign countries! Ask a guitarist to spend more than $500 for his instrument and watch him turn pale and start to sputter.

This is because we are spoiled. It *is* possible to get a playable, good sounding instrument for $500 or, for that matter, even $199. But, if we are to consider ourselves professionals, or even serious amateurs, we should not be afraid to spend $1000, $2000, or even $5000 if that is what it takes to get the sound that we seek.

Remember, the guitar is the first and most important link in your sound. You may be one of the lucky ones who finds an unplayed, salmon pink, 1962 Fender Stratocaster at a garage sale in Kansas for $125. If you are not, you should spend whatever it takes to get that ultimate tone.

VINTAGE AMPS

Vintage amplifiers are not in the same class as vintage guitars. This may be because Marshall is still, and Fender is once again, making good sounding amps.

Nevertheless, players still seek out older Marshall heads in search of that elusive sound that Clapton, Hendrix, and Van Halen seem to get. I have never been a Marshall user, so I cannot speak from direct experience. As a long-time Fender man, I can say that as good as the newer Fenders are, they cannot reproduce the incredible tone of an old, tweed 4x10 Bassman. Originally intended as a bass amp, it produces the sweetest guitar tone, both clean and distorted, you are likely to find anywhere.

Another highly-prized older amp is the Vox AC-30 tube amp. Mike Campbell *(Tom Petty and the Heartbreakers)*, Brian May *(Queen)* and many others swear by these.

Unlike vintage guitars, vintage amplifiers remain quite affordable. They can range from $250 for a pre-CBS blackface (refering to the color of the control panel) Fender Deluxe, to $600 or $700 for a tweed Bassman, a Fender Super Reverb, or Vox AC-30. An exception might be an older Marshall head that could fetch over $1000.

A few modern manufacturers have managed to duplicate the sound of these older amps. Jim Kelly's amplifiers combined the best of Fender and Marshall sounds in one unit. Unfortunately he is no longer in business, rendering these a kind of vintage amp as well. These units started at $1200 new, and may now be more, since they are no longer readily available. Howard Dumble makes amplifiers modeled on the best sounding Fenders, but they start at $2500.

With this in mind, vintage amps are starting to look like a real bargain. If you must have channel-switching and effects loops, these can be installed by many competent repairmen at a reasonable cost. Since the prices (at this writing) of vintage amps are not as inflated as their guitar counterparts, it is not as much of a concern to keep them in their original state.

VINTAGE EFFECTS

At first it may seem strange to be talking about vintage effects, until you realize that there are tube reverb and tape echo units that are close to thirty years old!

You could hardly help but notice that many of the effects mentioned in Appendix I are no longer being made. Why are artists, who can obviously afford the latest toys on the market, using gadgets that are hard to replace and often not as reliable their modern counterparts? The answer is, of course, *sound*.

Some of these artists developed their sounds when these were the only effects on the market, and are now unable to find a replacement that sounds quite the same. In fact, it is exactly this uniqueness of sound that makes guitarists seek out these units and put up with their quirks, their noise, and their unreliability.

One of the first companies to market a full line of effects was Electro-Harmonix. The goal of president Mike Matthews was to manufacture an affordable line of great sounding effects—and he succeeded. They tended to be noisy, not so much because of cheap manufacture or poor design, but because they were designed to leave the high frequencies in. Other manufacturers at the time were cutting off the top end to reduce noise.

Colorfully named units like the Big-Muff Fuzz and the Electric-Mistress Flanger were prized for a sound that remains unique to this day. The Deluxe Memory-Man Analog Delay with Chorus/Vibrato is still one of the best sounding analog delays around. And the most prized of all is the 16 Second Digital Delay. Other digital units have since come along that have longer delays and are quieter, but this unit remains unique in allowing the guitarist to record a line and then play it back—backwards!

Electro-Harmonix's chief rival at the time was the now equally defunct MXR. MXR effects were more reliable and roadworthy, being enclosed in cast metal cases (as opposed to E-H's flimsy housing), but few of their effects sounded as good. One exception was the Dyna-comp Compressor. These little red boxes have a unique sound that is highly valued by Adrian Belew and Andy Summers, as well as Nashville session legend Reggie Young (now reissued by Dunlop).

Other sought-after vintage effects are the Foxx Fuzz tone, old A/D/A Flangers, and tube Echoplex tape echoes. Old effects have not yet become highly inflated in price. They are, however, harder to find than either vintage guitars or amplifiers.

You will decide for yourself whether modern manufacturers can fullfill all of your sonic needs, or whether you must join the ranks of the vintage hunter-gatherers to obtain the elusive "tone of the gods."

BIBLIOGRAPHY

Guitar Gadgets by Craig Anderton, Amsco Publications,
  New York, London, Sydney
Guitar Gear edited by John Brosh, Quill/A Guitar Player Book
  New York

Guitar Player, Guitar World, Downbeat, and *Musician* Magazines are all good
sources for information on your favorite player's gear.

ABOUT THE AUTHOR

Michael Ross has been playing guitar for a long time. He has
played on both coasts of the United States, and in Iceland, Cuba,
England, and Puerto Rico. He has toured Norway with folk-singer Eric
Andersen and was creative consultant for the D.C.I. instructional video,
"Adrian Belew: Electronic Guitarist."

Ross currently resides in San Francisco with his wife, Nancy, and
their cat Simone, where he continues the search for the perfect guitar tone.

Hal Leonard Guitar RECORDED VERSIONS™ With Notes & Tab

Recorded Versions are terrific note-for-note guitar transcriptions of the hottest and biggest names in music — today and yesterday. Each Recorded Versions arrangement is accurately transcribed into standard notation and tablature so you can play the music of these artists exactly as they recorded it! Note-for-note, the hottest guitar product you can buy!

THE BEST OF GEORGE BENSON
Includes: Breezin' • Give Me The Night • Lady Love Me • On Broadway • plus ten more!   00699041 $9.95

CHUCK BERRY
Transcriptions and a review of Chuck Berry's music by Fred Sokolow. Includes: Back In The U.S.A. • Guitar Boogie • Johnny B. Goode • Mabellene • Roll Over Beethoven • more.
00692385 $12.95

CINDERELLA — NIGHT SONGS
Matching folio to the hit album: Night Songs • Shake Me • Nobody's Fool • Nothin' For Nothin' • Once Around The Ride • Hell On Wheels • Somebody Save Me • In From The Outside • Push, Push • Back Home Again.   00692375 $12.95

THE BEST OF ERIC CLAPTON
12 songs including: Cocaine • Lay Down Sally • Forever Man • Have You Ever Loved A Woman • more.   00692391 $12.95

DEF LEPPARD — HYSTERIA
Matching folio to the LP. 12 songs, including: Animal • Women • Hysteria.   00692430 $14.95

BO DIDDLEY GUITAR SOLOS
From Bo Diddley — one of the ''inventors'' of Rock 'n' Roll — here are eighteen of his biggest tunes transcribed directly off the recordings for guitar. You'll find detailed information about Bo Diddley's unique playing style — an amazing melding of Mississippi Delta blues, urban Chicago blues, '50s Rhythm and Blues plus space age electronics. Songs include: Bo Diddley • Diddy Wah Diddy • Hey! Bo Diddley • I'm A Man • Mona (I Need You Baby).
00692240 $14.95

IRON MAIDEN — POWERSLAVE/SOMEWHERE IN TIME
Matching folio to the albums ''Powerslave'' and ''Somewhere In Time.''   00693096 $17.95

IRON MAIDEN
Guitar transcriptions to all of the songs from their first four albums: Killers; Iron Maiden; The Number Of The Beast; Peace Of Mind. Formerly published by Cherry Lane. A real collector's item!
00693095 $19.95

LYNYRD SKYNYRD
A collection of their best, including: Free Bird • Gimme Three Steps • Whiskey Rock-A-Roller • and more.   00693412 $12.95

NIGHT RANGER — 7 WISHES
Matching folio to the hit album includes the hit singles ''Sentimental Street,'' and ''Four In The Morning.''   00693632 $9.95

PINK FLOYD EARLY CLASSICS
13 of their greatest hits including: Eclipse • Money • Saucer Full Of Secrets • Time • Us And Them.   00693800 $12.95

POISON — LOOK WHAT THE CAT DRAGGED IN
Matching folio to the LP: Cry Tough • I Want Action • I Won't Forget You • Play Dirty • Look What The Cat Dragged In • Talk Dirty To Me • Want Some, Need Some • Blame It On You • #1 Bad Boy • Let Me Go To The Show.   00693865 $14.95

THE BEST OF POLICE
Includes 19 transcribed arrangements: Every Breath You Take • King Of Pain • Synchronicity II • Roxanne • Wrapped Around Your Finger • and more.   00693864 $12.95

ELVIS PRESLEY
Elvis Presley brought the musicians and elements together to create the prototype rock band. The guitar solos in this book charted the course for rock and roll guitar. They were played by extraordinary lead guitarists — Scotty Moore, Hank Garland and James Burton — who were on the cutting edge of rockabilly, country and pop. 18 songs including: Heartbreak Hotel • Blue Suede Shoes • Hound Dog • Jailhouse Rock • more! Each song includes: tablature and music notation with chord grids and lyrics as well as playing tips. Also features a special section on the techniques of Scotty Moore, Hank Garland and James Burton.   00692535 $14.95

RATT — DANCING UNDERCOVER
Matching folio to the LP includes the songs: Dance • Enough Is Enough • Slip Of The Lip.   00693912 $16.95

RATT — INVASION OF YOUR PRIVACY
Matching folio to the hit album includes the hit single ''Lay It Down.''   00693910 $9.95

RATT — OUT OT THE CELLAR
Matching folio to the smash LP: Back For More • I'm Insane • In Your Direction • Lack Of Communication • The Morning After • Round And Round • Scene Of The Crime • She Wants Money • Wanted Man • You're In Trouble.   00693911 $14.95

GREAT ROCKABILLY GUITAR SOLOS
18 songs, transcribed note-for-note, as performed by these outstanding artists: Carl Perkins, Elvis Presley, Buddy Holly, Rick Nelson, Eddie Cochran, The Stray Cats and Ricky Skaggs. Includes such blockbuster Rockabilly hits as: Blue Suede Shoes • Hound Dog • Peggy Sue • Hello Mary Lou • Stray Cat Strut • Highway 40 Blues • and more!   00692820 $12.95

THE BEST OF U2
10 of their best, including: Gloria • Sunday Bloody Sunday • New Year's Day • Pride (In The Name Of Love) • more.
00694410 $16.95

U2 — THE JOSHUA TREE
Matching folio to the critically acclaimed smash LP. Includes: With Or Without You • Where The Streets Have No Name • I Still Haven't Found What I'm Looking For.   00694411 $14.95

YNGWIE MALMSTEEN — MARCHING OUT
Includes: Don't Let It End • Disciples Of Hell • I Am A Viking • I'll See The Light.   00694756 $14.95

YNGWIE MALMSTEEN — RISING FORCE
Matching folio to the smash LP: As Above, So Below • Black Star • Evil Eye • Far Beyond The Sun • Farewell • Icarus Dream Suite—Opus 4 • Little Savage • Now Your Ships Are Burned.
00694755 $14.95

YNGWIE MALMSTEEN — TRILOGY
Matching folio to the LP includes nine songs in note-for-note guitar transcriptions.   00694757 $16.95